CULTURAL DIFFERENCES

Read, Discuss, and Write

About the Authors

David and Peggy Kehe have been teaching ESL for over 30 years. In the 1970s they spent two years teaching EFL as Peace Corps Volunteers in Niger, West Africa. After that, they taught for a year on Lesbos Island, Greece; for twelve years in colleges in Japan; and for a number of years in colleges in the United States. Currently, in Bellingham, Washington, David teaches ESL, and Peggy is doing editing work. They both have MA degrees in Teaching ESL from The School for International Training in Brattleboro, Vermont. The cool greenery of rain forests serves as a backdrop for the lifestyle that they have established for themselves in the Pacific Northwest.

Other Pro Lingua Books
by David Kehe and Peggy Dustin Kehe

Write after Input
Writing Strategies One
Writing Strategies Two

The Grammar Review Book

Basic Conversation Strategies
Conversation Strategies
Discussion Strategies

For more information:
ProLinguaAssociates.com

CULTURAL DIFFERENCES

Read, Discuss, and Write

Exploring and Understanding Cultures Using Academic Skills

David Kehe
and Peggy Dustin Kehe

Pro Lingua Associates, Publishers
Pro Lingua Associates, Publishers
74 Cotton Mill Hill, Suite A 315
Brattleboro, Vermont 05301 USA
Office: 802-257-7779
Orders: 800-366- 4775
Email: info@ProLinguaAssociates.com
WebStore www.ProLinguaAssociates.com
SAN: 216-0579

At Pro Lingua
our objective is to foster an approach
to learning and teaching that we call
***interplay**, the **inter**action of language*
learners and teachers with their materials,
with the language and culture,
and with each other in active, creative,
*and productive **play**.*

ISBN 13: 978-0-86647-361-3; 10: 0-86647-361-0
Cultural Differences: Supplementary Activities
ISBN 13: 978-0-86647-362-0; 10: 0-86647-362-9

The illustrations: Except as noted, the illustrations in this book are from dreamstime.com agency: pages iii © Kolettt, 2 © Seamartini, 4 tsetse fly from Webster's New International Dictionary 1911, 4 © Lpd82, 11 © Darko Draskovic, 14 © Huating, 17 © Luisa Vallon Fumi, 19 © Szefei, 23 © Feverpitched, 24 © Zefart, 35 © Paop, 38 © Monkey Business Images, 41 © Isaxar, 43 © Goldenkb, 45 left © Andreblais, 45 right © Cecilia Lim, 46 © Danielal, 50 © Arne9001, 57 & 61 © Money Business Images, 64 © Paularesenko, 66 © Hongqi Zhang, 67 © Freud, 69 © Furtaev, 80 left © Valua Vitaly, 80 right © Szefei, 81 © Franz Pfluegl, 92 © Mycolors, 93 © Hongqi Zhang, 94 © Jkaryadi, 96 © Ngoc Dao, 107 © Scott Griessel, 110 © Maxim Tarasyugin, 111 left © Hanhanpeggy, 111 right © Wavebreakmedia Ltd, 112 © Hongqi Zhang, 118 © Jason Stitt, 121 left Paulwongkwan, 121 right Camille Tsang, 122 © Goldenkb, 123 © Artisticco Llc, 135 © Lee Snider, 136 © Jeffrey Banke, 137 © Littleny, 147 © Andres Rodriguez, 148 © Nikolay Mamluk, 151 © Ashwin Kharidehai Abhirama, 159 © Phartisan, 164 left © Tatyana Vycheyzhanina, 164 right © Jason Stitt, 165 © Atholpady, 169 © Radist, 170 © Michael Leung, 179 © Minerva Studio, 182 © Szefei, 184 © ishootRAW, 186 © Rohit Seth, 1989a © Jeffrey Banke, 198b & 198c © Mimagephotography, 198d © Netfalls, 198 lower © Ramzi Hachicho, 202 © Samrat35, 209 left © Leung Cho Pan, 209 right © Feverpitched. 211 © Carlosphotos. Cover design AA Burrows, Front cover photo © Kolettt, back cover photo © Elisseeva, wooden background @ Wirwarenlos.

Cultural Differences was designed by Arthur A. Burrows. It was set in Palatino, the most widely used, and pirated, face of the twentieth century, which was designed by Hermann Zapf in 1948 in Frankfurt. Although modern, it is based on Renaissance designs typical of the Palatinate area in Germany. The book was printed and bound by Royal Palm Press in Punta Gorda, Florida.

Printed in the United States of America
Seventh printing 2020. 1650 copies in print.

Contents

Introduction

Cultural Differences is designed to help high-intermediate to advanced students develop the skills that they will need to be successful in higher-level academic settings. In the process of studying about the reasons behind the norms in different cultures, ESL students develop reading, discussion, and writing skills. The materials are effective in a variety of academic ESL courses, such as in:

- an integrated academic-skills course
- a stand-alone reading and writing course
- a stand-alone discussion-skills course.

Cultural Differences is composed of two books. One book is the main text, which you are presently looking at, and it is composed of 14 units. Each unit includes a reading passage about cultural norms and the reasons for those norms. The exercises that follow the passages are divided into five parts:

Part 1: Study Guide questions

Part 2: Academic vocabulary exercises

Part 3: Preparation for discussion

Part 4: Academic writing techniques

Part 5: Preview questions for the next unit.

The second book, the ***Supplementary Activities***, contains additional materials. This photocopyable book is available as a separate book or available online at no charge at www.prolinguaassociates.com. Included in the ***Supplementary Activities*** are:

- Small-group discussion activities for each unit in the form of questions for Student A, Student B and Student C
- Whole-class discussion techniques and suggested procedures for implementing them
- Applied outside-of-class activities for each unit
- An answer key
- Quizzes.

As the title, **Cultural Differences: Exploring and Understanding Cultures Using Academic Skills**, implies, there are two educational aspects to the book.

1. Exploring and Understanding Cultures

Students learn about the norms in various cultures and the reasons why those norms differ from culture to culture. For example, in social situations, many Asians seem shy while Westerners seem more outgoing. Also, Americans tend to give more compliments to others than do Asians. There are good reasons for these differences, and this book discusses what the research into cultural differences has found. Because this content is particularly relevant to students' personal lives, they tend to find it enlightening and engaging. Students who have studied these materials have stated that the content provided them with a better understanding of their roommates, classmates, and instructors from other countries, and their host family members – and even of people from their own culture.

2. Using Academic Skills

Students develop academic reading, writing, vocabulary, and discussion skills.

Reading and Vocabulary Development. The reading passages are written in an academic style about research. They are similar to the type of reading assignments that students will have in academic courses. Each unit also contains Study Guide questions and academic vocabulary-development exercises.

Writing. To prepare students for the type of writing assignments they will encounter in academic courses, each unit includes specific techniques for developing paraphrasing skills, for writing reflection papers, and for writing essay answers to test questions. These specific writing techniques show students how they can delve more deeply into a topic and impress their instructors. The final units culminate in preparing students to write essays that incorporate information from sources.

Discussion. The discussion questions (available in the free online ***Supplementary Activities*** or as a separate photocopyable publication) are designed to help students engage in small-group and whole-class discussions. In order to maximize student participation in the discussions, the small-group questions are designated for Student A, Student B and Student C. Using the questions, the students interact with each other in a three-person discussion. These questions include two types: discussion about the content of the reading passages and discussion about students' personal experiences and opinions. In these discussions, the students have the opportunity to explain and to listen to classmates explain information from a passage in their own words, i.e., to paraphrase orally. This step helps students make a smooth transition to producing *written* paraphrases of their own.

Outside-Class Activities. Finally, each unit includes a culminating activity, "Applied outside-class interactions/observations," which can be found in the ***Supplementary Activities***. In these activities, students interview someone who is not a classmate about their experiences with that unit's cultural norms.

The ***Supplementary Activities*** also includes an answer key for each unit and quizzes for Units 1-3, 4-6, 7-9, 10-12 and 13-14.

A final note about the Study Guide questions: These questions for students are engaging yet do not burden the teacher with a lot of paper work (e.g. grading). The Study Guide questions and vocabulary exercises are designed to be checked by students themselves in small groups. If group members disagree about a correct answer, it presents an opportunity for them to refer back to the text and to collaborate in finding it. The teacher needs to intervene only when a group cannot agree, or wishes to double-check about whether they had truly arrived at a correct answer. The only assignments that the teacher would need to personally check are the exercises that introduce writing techniques.

An effective approach to using this material

1) Students are assigned to read a unit and write the answers to the Study Guide questions and vocabulary exercises. They also read the "Preparation for Discussion" questions.

2) In groups of three (or four), students are given the "Small-group discussion questions" (Student A, B, and C), which the teacher has photocopied from the ***Supplementary Activities***, and they participate in the discussion. In their groups, they also compare their answers to the Study Guide questions and vocabulary exercises.

3) The teacher conducts a whole-class discussion. Prior to the discussions in Units 1-5, the class is introduced to and practices a specific technique which they can use to be active members of a large-group discussion. During the whole-class discussion of the information in the unit, students try to apply these techniques.

4) Students are assigned the "Writing Technique" exercise for that unit.

5) In order to develop a schema for the next unit, students answer the preview questions.

6) Students are assigned the "Applied outside-class interactions/observations" activity (included in the ***Supplementary Activities***). While carrying out this activity, they take notes about what they have experienced. These notes can be given to the instructor, shared with classmates during small-group discussions, or explained during the whole-class discussions.

7) After completing three units, students take the quiz for those three units. These quizzes are included in the ***Supplementary Activities***.

On Third Person Pronouns

In this book, Pro Lingua Associates offers our solution to the vexing *he/she* problem. We have come to the conclusion that when a third person singular pronoun is needed and that person is indefinite (and hence the gender is unknown or unimportant), we will use the third person plural forms *they, them, their,* and *theirs*. We are aware that historically these forms represent grammatical plurality. However, there are clear instances in the English language where the third person plural form is used to refer to a preceding indefinite, grammatically singular pronoun.

Examples: *Everyone says this, don't they.*
Nobody agrees with us, but we will ignore them.

If you will accept the examples, it is not a major step to finding the following acceptable:

"The user of this book should find this easier because they can avoid the confusion and awkwardness of he *or* she *or* he/she *and the implicit sexism of using* he *for everybody."*

Long ago, English dispensed with *thee* and seems to be functioning quite well with two *yous*. So why not two *theys*?

Ray Clark, Senior Editor, Pro Lingua Associates

Cultural Differences

Read, Discuss, and Write

Acknowledgements

The authors would like to express their appreciation for the time that **Trish Navarre**, of Bellingham, WA, contributed to this material. Her recommendations were invaluable.
We would also like to thank **Kirsten Lutes**, also of Bellingham, for her many helpful observations.

Note:

Longman Dictionary of Contemporary English
http://www.ldoceonline.com/dictionary/
and *Cambridge Dictionaries Online*
http://dictionary.cambridge.org/dictionary/learner-english
were useful sources for definitions for the vocabulary exercises.

Section 1

Why Collectivists and Individualists Behave Differently

If you are a student from the West, for example from Europe or the U.S., perhaps you have noticed that people from the East, for example Asia or the Middle East, tend to do a lot of activities in groups. Also, people from the East may seem shy around strangers. Conversely, from the viewpoint of people from the East, people from the West appear to be independent, outgoing, and talkative, even among strangers. In Section 1 of this book, we will look at the reasons why people behave differently from each other.

Unit 1: Norms

Normal behavior in a culture

Reading

[1] An American professor was planning his first trip to India. He wrote a letter to the only Western-style hotel in Mysore, the city that he wanted to visit, asking for information about making reservations. He received a reply card that looked like this:

> Reservation date: May 15–21
>
> ___ We reserved a room for you for the dates above.
>
> X We are unable to provide a room for you for the dates above.

[2] After seeing the card, the professor assumed that the hotel had no rooms and made reservations at a different one. When he arrived in Mysore, he decided to check with that Western-style hotel in order to see if someone else had canceled a reservation. The desk clerk said that they had, in fact, been waiting for him to arrive. The professor showed the clerk the reply card with the "X" next to the line, "We are unable…." The astonished clerk said, "Of course there is an "X" there. We cross out the statements that do not apply." (Triandis, 1994b).

[3] Like this American professor, many of us assume that there is only one "natural" way to do something. However, once we begin having contact with other cultures, we soon realize that there are a variety of "right" ways to do almost everything.

[4] Researchers asked college students in several different countries to draw a map of the world in 10 minutes and to put in as many details as possible. Almost all the students drew their own country disproportionately large (Whittaker and Whittaker, 1972). This study reveals that it may be human nature to exaggerate how big one's own country is.

Similarly, people tend to believe that their own cultural beliefs and customs are the best or most natural. This tendency to view one's own group as superior to others is called **ethnocentrism**. We are likely to feel that the more another culture is similar to ours, the "better" it is. However, as we experience other cultures, we find that there are reasons why other people do things differently from us. As we saw from the example above about the reply card, the hotel in India had a system that worked well for them even though it was different from the system that someone from another country might use. Neither system was better or worse than the other, just different.

[5] Understanding different cultures is one of the most important needs in the world today. International students, educators, business people, government officials and travelers all experience new and different customs when they are in a foreign place. Depending on how well they understand those customs, they can find them either interesting and stimulating, or frustrating and painful. In fact, we will see how they have caused misunderstandings for friends, roommates, husbands and wives, teachers and students, employers and employees, and government officials. As one writer said, "Difficulties arise when behaviors considered polite and effective in one culture are seen as rude and inept in another" (Brislin, 2001, p. 214).

[6] The purpose of this book is to help you understand not only *how* cultures are different from each other but also *why* they are different. Cultures do not make customs just to be different from other cultures; instead, there are important reasons for these various customs. By understanding why people from different cultures behave differently from us, interact differently from us, have different perceptions, and express their emotions differently from us, we may be able to communicate better with people from all over the world.

[7] Let's begin our exploration of cultural differences with a survey that may help clarify what proper behavior in a culture is.

A Survey on Proper Behavior

Directions: Answer these questions about what people in your country consider to be proper behavior.

1. ***First names:*** Should people use other people's first names when talking to them? ______
2. ***Paying for others:*** If two people go out together (e.g., to a movie or a restaurant), should one of them offer to pay for the other one? ______
3. ***Birthdays:*** Should people send birthday cards and presents to each other? ______
4. ***Visiting:*** Is it all right for people to visit someone's home without telling the other person that they are coming? ______
5. ***Religion and politics:*** Is it all right to talk about religion and politics? ______
6. ***Anger:*** Is it acceptable for someone to show anger in public? ______
7. ***Affection:*** Is it all right for two people to show affection in public (e.g., by kissing or holding hands)? ______
8. ***Handshakes:*** Should people shake hands when they meet someone? ______
9. ***Money:*** Is it acceptable to talk about someone's own income and financial situation, and to ask others how much money they earn? ______
10. **Eye contact:** Should a person look directly in other people's eyes during a conversation? ______
11. ***Marriage:*** Is it acceptable for men to have more than one wife? ______
12. ***Tattoos:*** Is it acceptable for young people to get tattoos? _____
13. ***Babies:*** Should babies sleep in their parents' beds? ___
14. ***Boyfriends/girlfriends:*** Is it acceptable for a junior high school student to have a boyfriend or girlfriend? ______

Source: Argyle, Henderson, Bond, Iizuka, and Contarello, 1986.

[8] If you and someone from a different culture compare your answers to the questions above, it is likely that some of your answers will be different. Every culture has rules about how its members should or should not behave. These rules are called norms. Norms can be considered the "normal" way to behave, or the expected behavior. For example, driving a car on the right-hand side of the road is the norm in the United States and Canada, but driving on the left side is the norm in India and Hong Kong. In a number of American high schools, the norm is for students to wear casual clothes, such as blue jeans, but in a lot of other countries, wearing a uniform is the norm for that age group.

Tsetse Fly

[9] In a certain part of Africa, there used to be a great problem with an insect called the tsetse fly. The flies carried a disease which killed the cows. Without cows, there was no milk for babies, so mothers fed their infants their own milk for at least the first three years of a baby's life. However, if a woman gets pregnant, she will stop producing milk. As a result, it became taboo for women to have sex for the first three years after childbirth, so that she would not become pregnant. For this reason, it became acceptable for men to have more than one wife. In other words, polygamy became the norm for this culture (Triandis, 1994b). As we can see from this African example, there are reasons why different cultures have different norms (i.e., patterns of behavior.)

Cattle in Sardinia

[10] As mentioned above, norms are established by a group, and they specify how the group members should or should not behave. Interestingly, it's possible for the norms of a group to be different from the laws of a country. For example, there is a law against stealing in Italy. However, for cattle herders in Sardinia, in Italy, the norm allows for stealing in certain situations. In the Sardinian culture, equity is the norm, and these cattle herders would explain their norm by saying, "God wants everyone to have the same; when someone has more, we take it away (i.e., steal) to do God's work" (Triandis, 1994b, 100). This has been the norm for many centuries even though Italian law, in fact, prohibits stealing.

Part 1: Study guide for Unit 1

After you have read the information about the hotel reply card in ¶ *(paragraphs)* 1-2, read this:

You are planning to have a birthday party for your roommate. You send invitations to some friends of yours who have just arrived from India. They return the RSVP ("response") part of the invitation to you, and it looks like this:

> RSVP for the birthday party on October 15
> _X_ I will attend the party.
> ___ I will not attend the party.

1. Do you think your Indian friends will come to the party? ___
2. Explain your answer.

3. In ¶ 3, according to the first sentence, many people are apt to think that ___.
   a) there are many different, normal ways to do things
   b) there is one correct or normal way to do things

4. In ¶ 4, "disproportionately" means that each student drew their own country___.
   a) in the wrong place on the map
   b) as the only country in the world
   c) the wrong size compared to other countries

5. In ¶ 4, according to the "map" study, people are likely to ___.
   a) feel that their country is better than other countries
   b) feel that people all over the world are similar to each other
   c) feel that their country is worse than other countries

6. In the survey after ¶ 7, in Questions #2 and #7, there's the expression, "e.g." What does "e.g." mean? ("e.g." is an abbreviation for a Latin word.)
   a) in other words
   b) for example
   c) especially great

7. In your country, is it the norm to shake hands when you meet someone? _____
   What would happen if you did not follow this norm (i.e., shaking or not shaking hands)?

8. In ¶ 9, it mentions the word "taboo." Which one of the following situations do you think is considered taboo in most countries?
   a) A 22-year-old man who gets married to a 22-year-old woman
   b) A 25-year-old man who gets married to a 22-year-old woman
   c) A boy who gets married to his sister
   d) Not getting married

9. According to ¶ 9, why was it sometimes important that the women not become pregnant?
   a) Because this society didn't want to have too many children.
   b) Because if the women were pregnant, they wouldn't be able to produce milk for their babies.
   c) Because if the women were pregnant, there were diseases that could kill them.

10. The following is a paraphrase of ¶ 10. There are six mistakes underlined in the content, including "the government." Correct the mistakes by changing words and phrases.

a group

According to the paragraph, norms are made by the government, and they tell people in a culture how they are supposed to behave. In Italy, people are not allowed to steal because there is a norm against it. Nevertheless, in some parts of Italy, stealing cattle is the norm, and thus, it is acceptable in some circumstances. This is because they think that the government expects everyone to be treated equally. For example, if a rich man has 15 cows, and his poor neighbor has only one, the rich man can steal the cow from the poor man. This is a situation in which the norm for a group and the laws of a government are the same.

Part 2: Academic Vocabulary for Unit 1

Exercise 1: Words from context

In the chart below, in the right column, there are definitions of some words from Unit 1. In the middle column, at the top, notice the symbol "¶". That means "paragraph." You can find the word that has that meaning in that paragraph. Look in those paragraphs in the article and find the words that have these meanings. The first one is an example. (If you cannot find a word, ask your instructor to give you a first-letter hint.)

	Word	¶ *	Find the word that means . . .
1.	*assumed*	2	thought that some information was true without proof
2.		5	exciting; making you think in a new way
3.		6	talk or work together with someone
4.		6	a belief about something because it appears true
5.		10	says that something is illegal -- not permitted)

* **The symbol "¶" means paragraph.** You can find the word in that paragraph.

Exercise 2: Vocabulary Fill-in Exercise

Choose the words in Exercise 1 above to fill in the blanks below.

1. A quiet library is not a good place to go to __________ with your friends.
2. My cell phone wouldn't turn on, so I __assumed__ that the battery was dead.
3. Sending text messages is becoming popular, so our city ____________________ doing it when people are driving because it is dangerous.
4. Recently, we have been having some warm winters. Thus, people have the __________ that our climate is becoming hotter.
5. I always have ________________ conversations with Lee because he has had a lot of interesting experiences.

Exercise 3: Applied Vocabulary

The words in Exercise 1 above may appear below in a different form. For example, ***assumed*** could be ***assume, assuming***, or ***assumption***.

1. With whom did you interact before you came to class today? ________________
2. What do you think is the most stimulating type of movie (e.g., action, drama, Si-Fi, romance, documentary, comedy)? ____________________ Explain.
3. Which of the following is the correct way to use perception?
   a) Many people have the perception that the sun rises in the east and sets in the west.
   b) People in the West often have the perception that Asians are shy.
   c) There is a perception that January 1st is New Year's Day.
4. Write what you would assume if the following incidents happened to you:
   a) I look out of the window from my room, and I see a woman who is carrying an umbrella over her head. I would assume that ________________________________ ____________________
   b) I am walking down the street. A man in dirty clothes approaches me and asks me if I could give him some money. I would assume that ________________
   c) I am in class. All of my classmates are quietly reading. Suddenly, some of them shut their books, stand up, and start to put their books in the school-bags. I would assume ________________________________
5. Smoking cigarettes is prohibited in most high schools. What is something else that is prohibited in high schools?

Part 3: Preparation for discussion for the Introduction and Unit 1

Think about your answers to these questions. You do not have to write your answers.

1. Do you think that you are ethnocentric? In other words, do you think that your country is better than other countries? Explain your answer.

2. In ¶ 8, it mentions "norms" for how students should dress. Why do you think that some countries require students to wear uniforms?

3. Is polygamy taboo in your country?

4. In ¶ 9, in this example about the people in Africa, do you think that it is strange that polygamy is the norm? Explain your answer.

5. What is one custom from your country that you think would be good for other countries to have?

6. What is one custom from a different country that you think would be good for your country to have?

> ❖ **Note to teacher:**
> The "Small-group Discussion" questions are included here, in Unit 1, as an example. For all other units, the "Small-group Discussion" questions for groups of three (or four) in the form of separate pages for Students A, B, and C are available in the ***Supplementary Activities*** or can be downloaded free from-www.ProLinguaAssociates.com.

Small-group Discussion

Purpose

In many academic classes, group discussions are very common. These are good opportunities to impress your instructor. Instructors often will give a higher grade to students who try to participate well in group discussions. This activity will help you practice being an active group member.

Also, in many academic courses, students are required to write papers and take quizzes using information from sources (e.g., textbooks and articles). For these papers and quizzes, they need to be able to paraphrase information from the sources. In other words, you cannot just copy from the sources, but rather use your own words and style. In discussion groups, you will have the opportunity to discuss the content from the textbook in your own words and hear how others explain the ideas. After doing a discussions, it will be much easier for you to paraphrase information in papers and on quizzes.

And you can develop your speaking, pronunciation, and listening skills during discussions.

Procedure

In this discussion, you will be in groups of three or four students. One group member will be **Student A**, one will be **Student B**, and one (or two) will be **Student(s) C**. Each member will have different discussion questions. Student A will have questons 1, 4, 7, etc. Student B will have questions 2, 5, 8, etc. Student C will have questions 3, 6, 9, etc. Student A, you will read question 1. If your partners do not understand the question, you should re-read it or explain the question in different words. You should try to let your partners give the answer. If they cannot, you can give the answer. Student B, you will read question 2, and then Student C, you will read question 3, etc.

Small-Group Discussion for Unit 1

Do not write the answers. Do not look at your partners' pages.

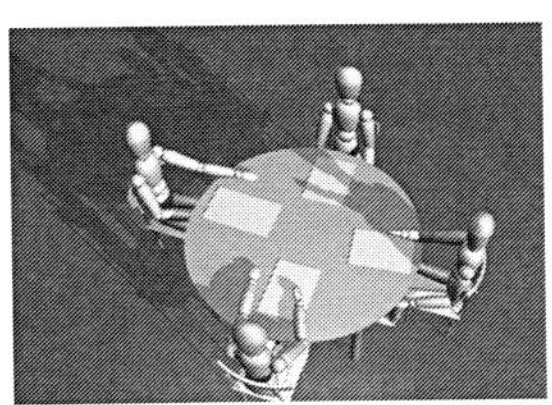

Student A

Directions

Read these clarification and discussion questions to your partners, and answer theirs.

1. Explain why the reply card confused the American professor in paragraphs 1 and 2.

4. Explain how the expression "ethnocentrism" is connected to the study about drawing maps in ¶ 4.

7. ***This is for discussion. All of us should respond.*** In ¶ 8, the article mentions "norms" for how students should dress. Why do you think that some countries require students to wear uniforms?

10. Explain what "polygamy" means in ¶ 9.

13. In ¶ 9, near the end of the paragraph, it says "i.e. patterns of behavior." What does "i.e." mean?

16. Let's check our answers to these:
1) Study guides on pages 5 and 6
2) Vocabulary exercises on paages 7 and 8

Note: ¶ is the symbol for paragraph.

Small-Group Discussion for Unit 1

Do not write the answers. Do not look at your partners' pages.

Student B

Directions

Read these clarification and discussion questions to your partners, and answer theirs.

2. In ¶ 1 and 2, did the clerk put the "X" on the wrong line? Explain.

5. ***This is a discussion question. All of us should answer this.*** Do you think that you are ethnocentric? In other words, do you think that your country is better than other countries? Explain your answer.

8. Explain the word "taboo" in ¶ 9.

11. ***This is for discussion. All of us should respond.*** Is polygamy a taboo in your country?

14. ***This is a discussion question. All of us should answer this.*** What is one custom from your country that you think would be good for other countries to have?

Note: ¶ is the symbol for paragraph.

Small-Group Discussion for Unit 1

Do not write the answers. Do not look at your partners' pages.

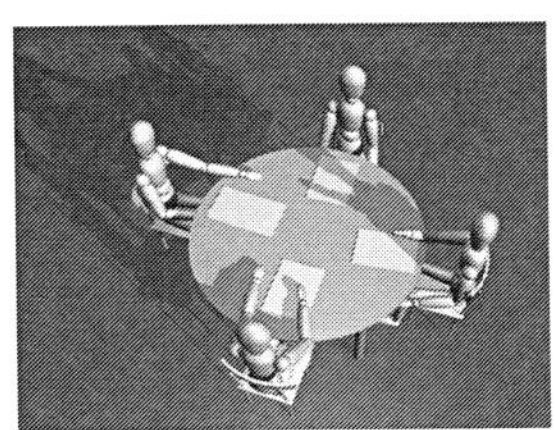

Student C

Directions

Read these clarification and discussion questions to your partners, and answer theirs.

3. In your country, how would hotel clerks mark this type of reply card?

6. Look at the survey on page 3 . Let's compare and discuss our answers.

9. Tell me if this is a taboo in your culture. You are standing in line to buy a ticket at a movie theater. Suddenly, a man walks from the back of the line to the front, and he buys his ticket. Would going to the front of the line be a taboo in your country?

12. ***This is for discussion. All of us should respond.*** In ¶ 9, in this example about the people in Africa, do you think that it is strange that polygamy is the norm? Explain your answer.

15. ***This is for discussion. All of us should answer this.*** What is one custom from a different country that you think would be good for your country to have?

Note: ¶ is the symbol for paragraph.

❖ For "Whole-class Discussion" techniques and a suggested procedure, see the *Supplementary Activities*, or download it free from www.prolinguaassociates.com.

❖ For "Applied Outside-class Interactions / Observations," see the *Supplementary Activities*, or download it free from www.prolinguaassociates.com.

Part 4: A technique for writing good answers on tests

Introduce your answers.

This is a technique that is useful when you are writing answers to quiz questions. When your instructors are reading your answers, it helps them know which question you are answering. Also, it helps you to focus on a question and to start writing your answer.

Exercise 1: Read this situation.

Situation

Wen is a Chinese student who had just started studying at an American college. After the first week of classes, he wanted to talk to his History teacher, so he went to her office. The door was closed, so he knocked twice and without waiting for a response, slowly opened it and walked in. The teacher looked surprised and a little upset (Cushner & Brislin, 1996).

Exercise 2: Analyze the style of students' answers about the *Test Questions*.

1) Read the *Test Question* in each box below.

2) Write the answers to the *Analysis Questions*.

Test Question 1: Why was the teacher upset at Wen?

Student A's answer:

Because Wen followed a different norm about opening a door to an office.

Student B's answer:

The reason why the teacher was upset was because Wen followed a different norm about opening a door to an office.

Analysis Question 1

Which student's answer is better because he introduced his answer by repeating part of the question? ___________________

Test Question 2: What do you think is the norm for opening doors in the instructor's culture?

Student C's answer:

The norm in the instructor's culture is probably to knock and then wait for an invitation to come in.

Student D's answer:

To knock and wait for an invitation to come in.

Analysis Question 2

Which student's answer is better because he introduced his answer by repeating part of the question? ___________________

Test Question 3: What does "upset" mean?

Student E's answer: Angry or irritated.

Student F's answer: Upset means angry or irritated.

Analysis Question 3

Which student's answer is better because he introduced his answer by repeating part of the question: ___________________

Exercise 3: In this exercise, you will practice introducing answers.

1) Read the exam questions below.

2) Choose a phrase from the box and fill in the blanks.

- ◆ In the story about the teacher and Wen
- ◆ This situation is interesting to researchers
- ✓ ◆ From the story about Wen
- ◆ The teacher felt
- ◆ The reason why Wen walked into the office

Exam question 1: What can we learn from the story about Wen?

Answer: ________________________________ we learned …

Exam question 2: Why is this interesting to researchers?

Answer: ________________________________ because …

Exam question 3: Explain what happened in the story about the teacher and Wen.

Answer: ________________________________, a Chinese student …

Exam question 4: How did the teacher feel when Wen entered her office?

Answer: ________________________________ irritated.

Exam question 5: Why did Wen walk into his teacher's office?

Answer: ________________________________ was because …

Exercise 4: Read this situation.

Situation

Betty was an American student who was studying at a university in Germany. Because of her high scores in German, she was able to get a scholarship. After the first week of classes, she joined several of her German classmates at a local restaurant. Some of them asked her about the U.S. policy on nuclear arms as well as about the American president's position on trade and immigration. Betty, who didn't read newspapers very much and was not interested in current events, was not prepared to discuss these topics and didn't say much. As a result, after that, she was not invited to join her classmates when they got together after class.

For German students, the norm is to discuss politics and foreign policy, and they expect their friends to be able to do the same. For the Germans, if someone doesn't participate in these discussions, they feel that that person is not very interested in them (Cushner & Brislin, 1996).

Exercise 5: Write answers to the questions about the information in the box above. Include introductions to your answers (which you practiced in Exercises 1, 2 , and 3 above). ***Write on other paper.***

1. What topics did the German students want to discuss?
2. Why didn't Betty participate very much during the discussion?
3. What does "current events" mean?
4. How do Germans feel if someone does not participate in a discussion about politics?
5. Do you think that Germans and Americans have different norms concerning discussion topics?

Part 5: Preview for Unit 2

Directions: Choose your answers to these questions.

1. Imagine this situation

You are four years old. You are in pre-school (or kindergarten), and you are sitting at a table next to another child. Your teacher gives you a plate with four pieces of your favorite food on it, and the teacher gives the other child a plate with only one piece of food. What would you do?

a) I would start eating my four pieces of food.
b) I would give some of my pieces of food to the other child.
c) I would give some pieces of food to the other child only if someone suggested that I should do that.

2. Imagine this situation

You are four years old. You are in pre-school (or kindergarten), and you are sitting at a table next to another child. Your teacher gives you a plate with only one piece of your favorite food on it, and the teacher gives the other child a plate with four pieces of food. What would you do?

a) I would start eating my one piece of food.
b) I would ask, or tell, the other child to give me some of their pieces.
c) I would take some pieces from the other child if they wouldn't give me any.

3. Think about your answers above and fill in the blanks

(You can write anything that you want in the blanks. There are no right or wrong answers.)

◆ I am ____

◆ I am ____

Unit 2
2.1: Collectivism and Individualism:
Determining which one you are

Reading

[1] When researchers studied the behavior of Asian and American children, they found a difference in the norm for sharing.

[2] In a study of American children (Birch and Billman, 1986), four-year-old children were paired with a friend. The pairs were seated at a table in a playroom. For each pair, the experimenter put a plate in front of one of the American children (the sharer) with 10 pieces of their favorite food. The other American child in each pair (the receiver) was given a plate with only one piece of food. The experimenter said, "I have some work to do in the other room. Stay here for a few minutes until I come back. You can eat now." The experimenter left, and the children were videotaped for five minutes.

[3] The researchers wanted to see if the sharer would give some of their 10 pieces of food to the receiver without any request by the receiver. This would be classified as "spontaneous sharing." If the receiver asked for some of the food, or just took some, it would be considered "elicited sharing." They found that among the American children in the study, spontaneous sharing was rare. The majority of the time, the receivers had to elicit sharing. They called attention to the inequality by saying, for example, "You have more than me." They made demands such as, "Give me some." Or they mentioned a positive or negative consequence, e.g., "I won't be your friend if you won't give me some."

[4] Rao and Steward (1999) replicated the American study that is described above with Chinese and Indian children. The researchers found that, in contrast to the Americans, the Asian children shared more frequently and shared more spontaneously than the Americans did. Also, unlike the Americans, who often refused to share even when their partner asked for some food, the Asian children never refused to share their food when their partner made a request.

[5] Why did the children from Asia and America behave so differently from each other? Cross-cultural psychologists have found that the norms for people who live in Asia are similar to those of people in Latin America and Africa but are different from the norms of people in Western Europe, Australia, Canada and the United States. Each culture can be categorized as either **collectivist** or **individualist**.

[6] Responding to the questions in the following questionnaire is a good starting point for gaining an understanding of the differences between collectivists and individualists.

Directions

Step 1: For each statement, circle a number on the scale from **1= Disagree to 9 = Agree**. When you respond, think of how you would answer these statements if you were *in your own country*.

Statements

1. If a relative told me that they needed money, I would help them as much as I could.
   Disagree 1 2 3 4 5 6 7 8 9 Agree
2. When I have a problem, I prefer to solve it myself, rather than follow the advice of others.
   Disagree 1 2 3 4 5 6 7 8 9 Agree
3. Before I get married, I will listen to my parents' opinion about the person whom I want to marry.
   Disagree 1 2 3 4 5 6 7 8 9 Agree
4. What happens to me is because of something that I myself did.
   Disagree 1 2 3 4 5 6 7 8 9 Agree
5. One of the pleasures of life is to be a member of a group.
   Disagree 1 2 3 4 5 6 7 8 9 Agree
6. The most important thing in my life is to make myself happy.
   Disagree 1 2 3 4 5 6 7 8 9 Agree
7. Parents who are elderly should live with their married children.
   Disagree 1 2 3 4 5 6 7 8 9 Agree
8. If I am working in a group but the group is going too slowly, it is better for me to leave it and work alone.
   Disagree 1 2 3 4 5 6 7 8 9 Agree
9. If I look for a job, I need one that has a group of co-workers with whom I can socialize outside of work.
   Disagree 1 2 3 4 5 6 7 8 9 Agree
10. If I want to do something excellently, I should do it myself, rather than in a group.
    Disagree 1 2 3 4 5 6 7 8 9 Agree
11. It is good for a child to continue the father's business.
    Disagree 1 2 3 4 5 6 7 8 9 Agree
12. If the company that I work for had money problems, and my boss asked me to take a lower salary, I would look for a different job.
    Disagree 1 2 3 4 5 6 7 8 9 Agree
13. I cannot be happy if my friends are unhappy.
    Disagree 1 2 3 4 5 6 7 8 9 Agree
14. It is very important for me to have an exciting and challenging life.
    Disagree 1 2 3 4 5 6 7 8 9 Agree

(adapted from Triandis, 1994b)

Step 2: Look at the numbers that you circled for Statements 1, 3, 5, 7, 9, 11, and 13. Add those numbers. Total = _____

Step 3: Look at the numbers that you circled for Statements 2, 4, 6, 8, 10, and 12. Add those numbers. Total = _____

If your total in Step 2 is higher, you tend to be more collectivist. If your total in Step 3 is higher, you tend to be more individualist. Which do you tend to be?

I am a/an ________________________.

7 Your score on the questionnaire above can show whether you have a tendency to be more collectivist or individualist. In general, researchers have found that East Asians and Latin Americans are more collectivist, while Canadians, Americans, and West Europeans are individualist. If you know anyone who scored higher on the odd-numbered questions, they probably have values and expectations that are different from someone who scored higher on the even-numbered ones. If a collectivist and an individualist work together at a company, are roommates, or get married, they might have conflicts unless they understand each other's differing value systems.

8 As mentioned above, some countries tend to have more collectivist characteristics and others more individualist ones. This does not mean that everyone in a particular country, for example China or Korea, is a collectivist or that everyone in the U.S. or Canada is an individualist. In fact, the authors of this book have found that international students from collectivist countries who are studying at colleges in the U.S. frequently have some individualist tendencies. Perhaps this could be true because the types of students who would leave their own countries to study in a foreign place tend to be more independent. Also, those collectivist students might have adopted some of the individualist values that they encountered while living outside their country, which could also happen to an individualist who is visiting a collectivist country. Another reason could be that, due to globalization, the differences between cultures are becoming less clear.

Individualism/collectivism rankings for 55 countries from most individualist to most collectivist

Most Individualist↓

1 United States	19 Israel	37 Hong Kong
2 Australia	20 Spain	38 Chile
3 Great Britain	21 India	39/42 Vietnam
4/5 Canada	22/23 Japan	39/42 West Africa
4/5 The Netherlands	22/23 Argentina	39/42 Singapore
6 New Zealand	24 Iran	39/42 Thailand
7 Italy	25 Russia	43 El Salvador
8 Belgium	26/27 Brazil	44 South Korea
9 Denmark	26/27 Arab countries	45 Taiwan
10/11 Sweden	28 Turkey	46 Peru
10/11 France	29 Uruguay	47 Costa Rica
12 Ireland	30 Greece	48/49 Pakistan
13 Norway	31 Philippines	48/49 Indonesia
14 Switzerland	32 Mexico	51 Colombia
15 Germany	33/35 East Africa	52 Venezuela
16 South Africa	33/35 Yugoslavia	53 Panama
17 Finland	33/35 Portugal	54 Ecuador
18 Austria	36 Malaysia	55 Guatemala

http://gert-hofstede.com/countries.html

Most Collectivist ↑

2.2: Collectivism and Individualism:

Group-oriented vs. self-oriented

9 Researchers asked people in two individualist countries (Australia and New Zealand) and in two collectivist countries (Japan and India) if they agreed with this statement: My goal is to do whatever I think is worth doing. The Australians and New Zealanders agreed 50% and 64% of the time respectively, while the Japanese and the Indians agreed only 32% and 12% of the time respectively.

[10] The central difference between collectivists and individualists is in how they view themselves. Collectivists sees themselves as part of a group; their goals and the group's goals are the same. Individualists view themselves as autonomous, or independent, from other people. If individualists don't like the goals of the group that they belong to, they will feel that it is preferable to leave that group and join a different one.

[11] This belief that individualists have that it is acceptable to leave a group and join another one starts at an early age. Researchers studied aggression among children who were between the ages of three and eleven in India, Japan, Kenya, Mexico, the Philippines, and the United States. They found that, compared to mothers in the other countries, which were all collectivist countries, the American mothers were less likely to discipline their children if they acted aggressively toward other children. For example, if their child wanted a toy that another child was holding and if their child just took it away from the other child, the American mothers would be less likely to tell their child that that is bad behavior and to return the toy to the other child. On the other hand, the Mexican mothers would be more apt to punish their child for such behavior. The researchers explain that the reason for this difference is because in Mexico, a collectivist country, there is a high level of inter-dependence, especially among members of the extended family. It's vital that

all members get along with each other because they might need each other's support in the future. In contrast, one American mother said, "If he can't get along with one child, he can always play with someone else" (Moghaddan et. al, 1993 p. 126, cited in Gardiner, 2001). For the Americans, people choose whom they want to have a relationship with, and these relationships can change at any time, so if someone doesn't like how another person behaved, they can just find new friends.

[12] Researchers asked individuals in different parts of the world to complete 20 statements that started with the words, "I am ...." People from collectivist cultures often completed the statements with words that implied membership in a group. For example, collectivists might answer, "I am a son," which is a member of a group (a family), or "I am a basketball player," which points to membership on a team. On the other hand, individualists more often answered with personal conditions and traits, for example, "I am happy," or "I am interested in soccer." In fact, in the study, students of Chinese or Japanese background gave twice as many group-related responses as they gave personal-trait ones (Smith and Bond, 1994).

[13] Interestingly, if we ask collectivists to describe themselves, they might not be able to do it unless we tell them the context. For example, if we ask them if they are friendly or outgoing or shy, they might answer differently, depending on the situation or context. They might say that they are outgoing around their family and friends but shy at a party with strangers. On the other hand, individualists would probably be able to describe themselves as being friendly, outgoing or shy in all situations (Smith and Bond, 1994).

[14] Researchers have found that when Koreans (who are collectivists) go skiing, they are more likely to ski in groups than Americans, who are individualists (Brandt, 1974). They also found that collectivists are more likely to eat in large groups, whereas individualists will eat in pairs or alone (Triandis, 1994b).

[15] Independence is very important to individuals. They are taught this value at an early age. Parents encourage their young children to make decisions. For example, when Jane was six years old, her mother asked her what she would like to do during the summer

vacation. Jane said that she'd like to either take gymnastic or ballet lessons, or learn a musical instrument. A week later, she told her mother that she had decided to learn how to play the piano. Individualist parents also expect their children to leave home after they have finished high school. When the children are trying to decide whether or not they want to go to college, or what college to attend, or what career to pursue, they tend to make those decisions based on their own desires rather than on the preferences and expectations of their family members. This does not mean that individuals do not like to be members of a group. They do join groups, but they might not do everything that the group wants them to do.

16 On the other hand, collectivists feel a strong obligation and responsibility to their families and to their other groups. When making decisions, they consider others' needs and expectations. This attention to others' needs was examined in a study that researchers conducted with Japanese and American children. In a learning activity, if the child made a correct response, sometimes the experimenter gave a piece of candy to the child as a reward, and sometimes the experimenter himself took a piece of candy as a reward. The researchers found that the American children learned more effectively when they themselves were rewarded with the candy, but the Japanese children learned equally well whether they themselves received the reward or whether the experimenter received it. The researchers explained that the behavior of the Japanese children is rooted in early childhood training. Japanese mothers often reward their children's good behavior by saying, "I am happy"; and they respond to bad behavior by saying, "I am sad." Thanks to their mothers' expressions of happiness and sadness, even at a young age, Japanese children are forming an awareness of how their actions affect the feelings of others (Haruki, et. al, 1984 referred to in Triandis, 1994b).

17 At the same time that collectivists are trying to help others, they are reassured that their families will always be willing to help them when they need it. Sometimes this interdependence among family members can lead to nepotism, i.e., situations in which a person is given a job or promotion because of their family connections rather than because of their ability. In collectivist countries, nepotism is not only considered acceptable, it is often expected (DeCapua, 2004). For example, if someone is elected mayor of a city, they will "take care of" their children, their brothers and sisters, and/or their nephews and nieces by giving them positions in their government. In contrast to this, in some individualist countries like the United States, it's illegal for government officials and others who have powerful public positions to hire a family member.

Part 1: Study guide for Unit 2

1. Fill in the blanks with the words ***sharer*** or ***receiver*** about the experiment of the four-year-olds in ¶ 2-4.

   a) The ________________ received 10 pieces of food.
   b) The ________________ received one piece of food.
   c) The ________________ in the American study asked the ____________ to give them some of their food.
   d) The ________________ in the Asian story frequently gave some of their food to the ________________ .

2. Read the dialog. Write ***Asians*** or ***Americans*** in the blanks.

Situation 1

Receiver: Give me some of your food.
Sharer: No.

These children are probably ________________ .

Situation 2

Receiver: I have only one piece of food.
Sharer: Here. You can have some of mine.

These children are probably ________________ .

3. Fill in the blanks with the names of the countries.

◆ Australia ◆ Brazil ◆ Canada ◆ China ◆ U.K.
◆ France ◆ Germany ◆ India ◆ Indonesia ◆ Japan
◆ Korea ◆ Mexico ◆ New Zealand ◆ U.S.A

Collectivist countries: ________________ ________________
________________ ________________ ________________
________________ ________________

Individualist countries: ________________ ________________
________________ ________________ ________________
________________ ________________

4. In ¶ 7, it mentions ***values*** and ***value systems***. Circle the letters of the examples of ideas that could be part of a value system. (Choose 9)

A) A good person shares things with others.
B) The sky is blue.
C) Children should get advice from their parents.
D) We ought to get a variety of experiences in life.
E) A good computer can be easy to use.
F) It is best if people tell their opinions directly to others.
G) Last night, she studied from 7:00 p.m. until midnight.
H) If you have weak eyes, you should wear glasses for reading.
I) We should work hard.
J) It is necessary for women to stay home and take care of their children.
K) Every family should have a son.
L) My watch cost $500.
M) It is important that people be treated equally.
N) Islands are popular places for people on vacation.
O) We should be allowed to have quiet time by ourselves.

5. Look at the study in ¶ 9. Fill in the blanks with how often people agreed with this statement: My goal is to do whatever I think is worth doing.

Japanese = _____% Indians = ____%
Australians = _____% New Zealanders = _____%

6. Ken belongs to a rock band with four other musicians. One day, the other members decide to change from playing rock to jazz. Ken, who prefers rock music, decides to quit the band and start a new one. This shows that Ken feels that he is ___. (Choose one.) (See ¶ 10.)

a) autonomous from others
b) dependent on others

7. In question #6 above, Ken is probably from ___. (Choose one.)

a) a collectivist society
b) an individualist society

8. In ¶ 11, it mentions "extended family." Which of these is an example of an extended family?

   a) a mother, father and two children
   b) a mother, father, two children, a grandmother, aunt, uncle and three cousins
   c) a mother, father, two children, a grandfather, aunt, and three neighbors

9. This question is related to ¶ 12. Identify each of the following by writing ***collectivist*** or ***individualist*** in the blank after each one.

   a) I am a student at Northeastern High School. ____________________
   b) I am interested in watching movies on the weekend. ______________
   c) I am 20 years old. ______________________________
   d) I am a manager of an Internet company. ____________________

10. Imagine that you are the manager of a company, and you need to hire a clerk. Which of these is an example of nepotism? (See ¶ 17.)

    a) You interview three men and two women for the job and hire one of them.
    b) You don't interview anyone, but instead, you hire your uncle.

11. Write one clarification question about a word, sentence, or idea that you do not understand in this unit. (If you understand everything, pretend that you don't.)

Part 2: Academic Vocabulary for Unit 2

Exercise 1: **Words from context**

Look at the paragraphs listed in the middle column of the chart below to find the words that have the meanings in the column on the right.

	Word	¶ *	Find the word that means . . .
1.		3	unplanned
2.		3	an event that happens as a result of another event that happened
3.		7	arguments or disagreements
4.		12	indirectly suggested something
5		15	chase or try to achieve something

* **The symbol ¶ means paragraph number.** You can find the word in that paragraph.

Exercise 2: Vocabulary Fill-in Exercise

Choose the words in Exercise 1 above to fill in the blanks below.

1. My parents were very strict when I was younger, so we often had ______________ when I wanted to do something that they didn't allow.
2. On the first day of summer vacation, when I sat down for breakfast, I noticed that my father had put a newspaper next to my plate. It was open to the "Help Wanted" section. By doing that, my father ______________ that he wanted me to find a job.
3. The news reported that a famous rock band would arrive at the airport at noon. Suddenly, 50 fans appeared at the airport. It was a ______________ action by their fans.
4. Juan and Marina want to find the best place to live. They ______________ this goal by traveling all around the world on their vacations.
5. One ______________ of playing computer games at 2:00 a.m. is that you will feel tired the next day.

Exercise 3: Applied Vocabulary

1. Write ***a spontaneous*** or ***an elicited*** in the blanks.
   a) You are walking along the street in a city. A homeless person approaches you and says, "Could you give me some money so I can get something to eat?"
   This is an example of ______________ action.
   b) You are walking toward a building. You notice a man in front of you who is carrying a huge box, and he is about to enter the building. You quickly pass him in order to open the door for him.
   This is an example of ______________ action.
2. With whom have you had a conflict recently (e.g., parents, boss, a girlfriend, a roommate)? ______________ Briefly tell what the conflict was about.
3. What could be a negative consequence of sending a text message while driving a car?
4. Let's say that you painted a picture and showed it to me. If I laugh and say, "I know a five-year-old child who can paint better than you," what did I imply?
   a) You are a good painter.
   b) You are a bad painter.
   c) I know a child who is a good painter.
5. What job are you planning to pursue in the future?

Part 3: Preparation for discussion for Unit 2

Think about your answers to these questions. You do not have to write your answers.

1. If you were a four-year-old in the experiment with the pieces of food, would you behave more like an American or Asian child as a receiver and sharer? Explain your answer.
2. When you were a child, did you treat your friends equally? Were there some children whom you did not like very much so you didn't treat well? Or did you treat them well even though you didn't like them very much? Give some examples.
3. Are you surprised that you tend to be a collectivist or individualist? Explain your reason.
4. In general, are your goals similar to individualists' or collectivists' goals?
5. Imagine that you have a boyfriend or girlfriend whom you would like to marry. If your parents said that they didn't want you to marry this person, would you still marry them? Explain.
6. In ¶ 15-16, it discusses independence. Do you think that your family has treated you more like a collectivist or individualist concerning independence? Give some examples.
7. In ¶ 17, it mentions nepotism. Is this common in your country? Do you feel it causes problems or is it a good system? Give some examples.

❖ For "Small-group Discussion" questions in the form of Students A, B, and C, see ***Supplementary Activities***, or download it free from www.ProLinguaAssociates.com.

❖ For "Whole-class Discussion" techniques and a suggested procedure, see the ***Supplementary Activities***, or download it free from www.prolinguaassociates.com.

❖ For "Applied Outside-class Interactions/Observations," see the ***Supplementary Activities***, or download it free from www.prolinguaassociates.com.

Part 4: A technique for writing good answers on tests

Use your own words to explain information from a source.

When you write an academic paper that includes information from a source, for example, a book, academic journal, or the Internet, it's important that you don't just copy from the source. You should explain that information using your own words and style. In other words, you should paraphrase the information.

Exercise 1: Read "A student's paragraph" below, which a student wrote in an essay about learning a foreign language.

A student's paragraph

Learning a foreign language is a challenge. In my school, we studied reading, writing, speaking and listening in the same class. I learned to read well but not to speak. Aside from this caveat, the integration of the four skills is the only plausible approach to learning a foreign language.

Exercise 2: Look at the style and vocabulary of the sentences in the paragraph above. Underline the sentences which you think the student possibly copied from a source (e.g., from a book or the Internet).

About Plagiarism

It's very easy for instructors to know when an ESL student plagiarized (copied) from a source because the style and vocabulary level is often different from the student's usual style and level. The last sentence is obviously copied from a source. A good paraphrase would have been this: There were problems with this type of class. However, teaching all four skills in one class is the best method.

In the next exercises, you will practice using your own words and style.

Exercise 3

1) Read this "Information from a source" and the Sample Test Question under it.
2) Read Student A's and Student B's answers.

> ***Information from a Source***
>
> "Members of Asian cultures see themselves as inherently connected with others" (Lonner and Malpass, 1994).

> ***Sample Test Question:*** How do Asians view themselves?
>
> ***Student A's answer:*** Asians see themselves as inherently connected with others.
>
> ***Student B's answer:*** Asians see themselves as naturally part of a group.

Exercise 4: Look at the Sample Test Question and students' answers in Exercise 3 above. Choose the correct answers below.

1. Which student copied from the source: ***Student A*** or ***Student B***?
2. Which student explained the source information using different words: ***Student A*** or ***Student B***?
3. Which student's answer is better: ***Student A*** or ***Student B***?

When you explain information from a source, you should not use words that are **not common** for you. Those are words that you would **not normally** use when you write an essay.

Exercise 5: Underline the words and phrases that are **not common** for you to use in your own essays.

1. *(Example)* Individualists express their dissonant views very clearly.
2. *(Example)* The child was sallow and glum with a swollen belly and listless eyes.
3. The task is to divert or eliminate these unnatural cognitive processes.
4. People often attribute success to their own astuteness.
5. A major antecedent of individualism is affluence.
6. Mr. Dean's boss has preposterous ideas that almost always flop.

Exercise 6

Choose the words or phrases to complete the paraphrased sentences.

- ◆ frightened
- ◆ bad teachers
- ✓◆ poor grades
- ◆ very interesting
- ◆ fail
- ✓◆ more help
- ◆ This report is the top

1. *(Source)* The school will provide extra assistance for low-achieving students.
   (Paraphrased) Students who are getting poor grades can get more help from the school.

2. *(Source)* The news is hitting the headlines.
   (Paraphrased) ______________________ story on the TV, Internet and in the newspapers.

3. *(Source)* The results are absolutely fascinating.
   (Paraphrased) These are ______________________ results.

4. *(Source)* The air-turbulence caused alarm among the airplane passengers.
   (Paraphrased) The passengers were ______________ by the movement of the plane.

5. *(Source)* It is a failed educator who resorts to flunking his students.
   (Paraphrased) The reason why some students ______________ is because of ______________________

Exercise 7

Complete the paraphrased sentences with your own words.

1. *(Source)* The company goes out of its way for its employees.
   (Paraphrased) The company tries very hard to help its workers.

2. *(Source)* The elderly lady was extraordinarily prosperous.
   (Paraphrased) The old woman was ______________________

3. *(Source)* When checking into a hotel, travelers should avoid accepting an accomodation on the first floor because it may be easily hit by a burglar.
   (Paraphrased) Hotel guests should ______________________
   ____.

4. *(Source)* Companies which permit employees to bring their pets to work have found that the pets are responsible for helping to develop a stress-free work situation and for encouraging employees to interact with each other more.

   (Paraphrased) Some companies allow ____
   ____
   ____.

5. *(Source)* When they have a naughty child, some parents believe that spanking is the only way to deal with the situation.

   (Paraphrased) Some parents spank their children because ____________________
   ____

6. *(Source)* Young people often don't realize the negative consequences of drunk driving.

   (Paraphrased) Often teenagers drink and drive because ____________________
   ____.

Part 5: Preview for Unit 3

Directions: Write your answers to these questions.

1. When you were in high school, did you belong to many clubs or teams, or did you belong to only one or two, or no clubs or teams? ____________

2. When you are in your country, do you feel lonely sometimes? _______

3. Since you were born, has your family moved from your home to a different place, or has your family stayed in the same place? _________

Unit 3

3.1 Reasons for the norms in collectivist cultures:

Needing to work together

Reading

[1] Societies in many parts of Asia, Africa and Latin America, are considered "simple." This means that, in general, the main occupation is farming, and people depend on their family members, friends, and neighbors to survive. If there is a natural disaster like a flood or a drought that kills the crops, they know that community members will share their food. Because, generally speaking, the people in these agrarian societies do not have much money, they usually live their whole lives in the place where they were born. As a result, these people know each other well, have common goals, and need to get along with each other. On the other hand, some parts of Asia, Africa, and Latin America are no longer "simple" or poor; instead, many of the people are financially comfortable and live in large cities. However, even though they might look like Western-style individualists, they remain collectivists because they have maintained their identity with their group and do not see themselves as individuals who are separate from others (Triandis, 1994b).

[2] For collectivists, cohesiveness and harmony among group members are most important, but for individualists, independence and freedom are vital. For collectivists, the worst thing that could happen to them is to be excluded from their group. For individualists, the worst thing is to feel obliged to depend on other group members or to conform to a group (i.e., to do what a group tells them to do, or to act like other group members) (Triandis, 1994b). The following true story could further illustrate the difference. Two Americans were living in an Asian country. It was early May, and even though it was spring according to the calendar, the temperatures would sometimes be cold. At work, they noticed one of their Asian colleagues who arrived wearing a thin sweater and shivering with cold. They asked her why she hadn't worn a heavy coat that cold morning, and she responded, "I wanted to, but it's spring now, and I knew that people in my neighborhood

would give me strange looks if I wore a winter coat today." In other words, she was concerned that people might disapprove of her. The American staff-members, on the other hand, didn't hesitate to wear their winter coats, hats, and gloves to work that spring morning even if they were the only ones who were wearing heavy clothes. (This was a personal experience of the authors of this book.)

3.2 Reasons for the norms in Individualist cultures:
Less need for a support group

3 In Canada, the United States, Western Europe, and Australia, societies are "complex," which means that there are a variety of different jobs for people to choose from, besides farming. The people are, in general, more affluent than in collectivist cultures, and because of this, they feel more independent. This makes it easier for them to move away from their families, friends, and neighbors if doing so fits their goals and desires. In other words, because individualist societies are relatively wealthy, people can move to a place that is far away from their relatives and friends and find a job fairly easily. If they need help, for example, they need someone to take care of their children while they are working, they usually have enough money to pay for that kind of service. As a result, people do not identify with one group, but instead see themselves as individuals with their own goals. Nevertheless, this independence can cause problems for some individualists. A study found that 26% of Americans reported that they felt lonely, an emotion that is uncommon in collectivist countries (Triandis, 1990).

3.3 In-groups:
People who affect our behavior

4 An important concept in Cross-Cultural Psychology is the in-group. Imagine a teenager named Tony. Tony belongs to a gang, which is his most important in-group. He sees himself as a gang member; in other words, he doesn't think of himself as a good student or as an athlete. His in-group, i.e. his gang, influences his actions because he wants to behave in a way that will assure that he will continue to be accepted by the other members. He has tattoos, he wears his gang's style of baggy clothes, and he is willing to fight to protect his gang's territory. Now imagine Ken, whose situation is very different from Tony's. His most important in-group is his family, including his aunts, uncles and cousins. Needless to say, Ken dresses and behaves quite differently from Tony because of the influence of his in-group. As we can see from the situation of Tony and Ken, an in-group is a group of people whose norms, goals, and values shape the behavior of its members. Collectivists like Ken consider people who are concerned about their happiness and who give

them support, for example friends and family, to be their in-group members. Individualists, like Tony, consider their in-group members to be people who agree with them about important issues, and who share the same values (Triandis, 1990). It's important to note here that individualists can consider family members to be part of their in-group as long as those family members share the same values. Similarly, collectivists can have people outside their family as an in-group as long as they give them support and look out for their happiness.

5 Collectivists are very close to the members of their in-group. Thus, it is difficult for someone who is not a member of the in-group to become close to them. However, if someone who is not a member of the in-group becomes close to a collectivist, it's easy to get to know them and they might be surprised at the types of questions they will be asked. For example, a collectivist friend might ask questions that individualists would not ask even of their closest in-group friends. Collectivists might ask, "How much money do you make?" or "What kind of sex life do you have?" On top of that, once a person becomes close to a collectivist, the collectivist will make sacrifices to maintain the friendship.

6 Unlike the situation with collectivists, it is easy to become friends with individualists. However, the individualists will continually evaluate whether the relationship has benefits for them. Regarding any relationship, the individualists tend to ask themselves questions like "What value does this relationship have for me?" If a relationship (with anyone—either another individualist or a collectivist) begins to feel like a burden, the individualist will probably end it (Triandis, 1994a).

3.4 In-groups:
Close vs. casual relationships

7 Every year in American high schools, a yearbook is published with the pictures of all the students and the names of clubs and groups that each student belonged to during that school year, e.g., Drama Club, the basketball team, Chess Club, or the band. Most students take pride in having a long list of activities next to their picture.

8 On the other hand, in collectivist cultures, a student may be encouraged to join just one club and give full attention and loyalty to that one group. The collectivist student will spend a lot of time with that club and develop a close relationship with its members.

9 In Japan, when people interview for a job, the interviewer often asks them about *the* (one) club that they belonged to. The interviewer is interested in learning about how hard the applicants worked for that club, how loyal they were, and how well they got along with the other club members. Job interviewers in the United States, on the other hand, look for applicants who have a wide variety of skills and interests; as a result, they expect applicants to talk about the many activities that they are interested in and the large number of clubs that they have belonged to (Brislin, 1994).

10 For individualists, the relationship among in-group members tends to be casual. They are more likely to talk about the weather, sports, or politics rather than about their personal lives, their future plans, their problems, or their financial situation. It would be unusual for an individualist to call a friend at 2:00 a.m. to explain that he couldn't sleep because he was worried about a problem and wanted to talk to someone about it. One reason for this is because individualists have a wide range of people in their in-groups, so they wouldn't have time to talk to all the friends who might have a problem at 2:00 a.m. Therefore, individualists' relationships are often casual and they tend to talk about lighter topics, such as weather and sports, rather than about their hopes and problems. On the other hand, a collectivist feels that it is important to be a "good friend" and will make sacrifices for other in-group members (Triandis, 1994b).

11 Collectivists tend to have only a few in-groups; sometimes a person from a collectivist culture has only one in-group, such as their extended family and friends of their family. In many Asian countries, the family and neighborhood that a person is born into, or the company they work for, or the school they attend, will determine that person's in-group. In other words, they don't choose their in-group, but members try very hard to do whatever is necessary to keep the in-group united.

12 For a collectivist, the in-group is extremely important. Because collectivists do not often move to new areas, they tend to keep the same in-group for many years or for a lifetime. For this reason, the members try to maintain harmony and to avoid conflicts among themselves. Each member tries to do what the group expects. They see themselves as a component of a complete picture, not as individuals. In traditional areas of Indonesia,

people do not even use personal names like "Tom" or "Mary"; rather, they use teknonyms (words that indicate their position in a family), for example, "the oldest son of the Smith family" (Lonner and Malpas, 1994). Teknonyms are only one way that, in collectivist societies, members of an extended family learn from childhood what their position is in relation to other members. They know to whom they must show respect, at whom they can yell, and to whom they can talk about a problem. In sum, relationships play an important role in everyone's life, and teknonyms serve as a specific description for each relationship. In individualist cultures, where specific relationships do not affect one's behavior as much, a brother-in-law could be, for example, "my wife's brother," "my sister's husband," or "my wife's sister's husband." However, in India, a collectivist society, Hindus have a specific word for each of these. "My wife's brother" is called *salaa* and "my sister's husband" is *bhanoi*, and "my wife's sister's husband" is *saandu-bhai*. They even have a name for "my mother's brother's daughter-in-law's son" (Laungani, 2007).

13 A collectivist behaves differently toward someone, depending on whether that person is a member of their in-group or a member of an out-group. The following example illustrates this. An American who has close connections to Greece sometimes calls a business there. If the secretary who answers the phone is a traditional Greek, she will answer the phone by asking, "What do you want?" This can sound rude. After the American explains that he is related to her boss or is a friend of the boss, she will quickly change how she speaks and will say something more friendly, for example, "How lovely to hear your voice" (Triandis 1996). In individualist cultures, on the other hand, people are less likely to behave very differently when interacting with members of their in-group or an out-group.

14 Expectations about helping in-group members can cause problems when individualists and collectivists interact. Bristlin (2001) tells the story about an American professor, Dr. Jack Douglas, who was teaching at Beijing University in China. During his time in China, one of the Chinese professors, Dr. Zhou Chao, was especially helpful by introducing him to important people, helping him with his research, and entertaining him during his free time. After a period of time, Dr. Douglas returned to the U.S., and one day he contacted Dr. Chao in order to tell him that he needed to hire a research assistant, and asked Dr. Chao if he had any recommendations. Dr. Chao immediately recommended Ms. Wang, who was a colleague at Dr. Chao's school. Dr. Douglas thanked him for the recommendation and said that he would consider Ms. Wang in addition to some other people who had applied for the position. A few weeks later, Dr. Chao was disappointed when he heard that Dr. Douglas had chosen a different person for the research assistant. In fact, he felt betrayed. At the same time, Dr. Douglas was surprised and hurt when he heard about Dr. Chao's reaction.

15 Brislin explains the reason for this misunderstanding between Dr. Chao and Dr. Douglas. For an individualist like Dr. Douglas, it's important to follow one's own goal, which, in this case, was to find the most qualified person. He advertised the position, carefully looked at the qualifications of the applicants, and tried to choose the best. On the other hand, Dr. Chao, a collectivist, considered his goals and the goals of his in-group to be the same. In this case, he was trying to take care of an in-group member, Ms. Wang. In addition, in China, there is a custom of favor exchanges. Because Dr. Chao had helped Dr. Douglas when he was in China, he felt that Dr. Douglas should repay the favor by hiring Ms. Wang.

Part 1: Study guide for Unit 3

Questions 1-6 are about ¶1-3. Write ***collectivists*** or ***individualists*** in each blank.

1. If ______________________ were excluded from their group, it is possible that they might "die."

2. If ______________________ were excluded from their group, they might look for another one.

3. If ______________________ lost their house and job because of a natural disaster, they would look for a new situation.

4. If ______________________ lost their house and job because of a natural disaster, their family and friends would help them.

5. My father and brother work 48 hours a week, so I think that I should do the same. My grandparents live with my family, and I think that my parents should live with me when they get old. I am probably ______________________ .

6. My father and brother work 48 hours a week, but I want to enjoy life more, so I plan to work only 36 hours or so. When my parents get older, I'll decide at that time whether to take care of them in my home. I am probably ______________________ .

7. According to ¶ 2, the story of the woman who didn't want to wear a coat on that cold morning is an example of ___.

   a) a collectivist who did not want to be excluded from her group
   b) an individualist who did not want to be forced to conform to her group

8. After reading ¶ 4, write ***Tony*** or ***Ken*** next to what are probably their norms or values.

_______ a. It's natural to do homework for four hours every night.

_______ b. It's natural to never bring books home to do homework.

_______ c. It's natural to ride around in a car until 2:00 a.m.

_______ d. It's natural to go to a restaurant with the family once a month.

_______ e. A college education is valuable.

_______ f. Carrying a knife is necessary in case a fight happens.

Questions 9-11 are about the term *in-group*.

9. Are my co-workers an in-group for me? _________

I work part-time at a fast-food restaurant. When the manager isn't at work, my co-workers like to joke around, take long breaks, and secretly eat food. I, however, prefer to work seriously and not eat any food.

10. Are my teammates an in-group for me? _________

I'm on a basketball team. When we are on a bus on our way to a game, my teammates like to play cards and talk. I prefer to listen to music on my headphones. After a game, my teammates usually go to a hamburger shop together, but I go straight home. My teammates have short hair, but mine is long.

11. Are Tom and Sue an in-group for me? _________

I used to hate jazz, but recently I met Tom and Sue, who both love jazz. Now I go to jazz clubs with them and even buy jazz online. They both can play musical instruments, so I started taking piano lessons.

12. Re-read ¶ 7-9. Which statements summarize that section?

    a) Collectivists probably know a little about many people, but individualists probably know a lot about a few people.

    b) Collectivists are expected to have a wide variety of general experiences, but individualists are expected to have narrow--but more intense--experiences.

    c) High schools in individualist countries probably offer more clubs than high schools in collectivist countries.

    d) Close relationships with others are probably considered more important in collectivist cultures, whereas a variety of experiences is considered to be of great value in individualist cultures.

13. Identify which of these people, Person A or Person B, is probably ***a collectivist*** and which is ***an individualist***.

    Person A's in-group members: his parents and sister; his grandparents, uncles, aunts, cousins; five close friends from elementary school whom he has known for 10 years; his father's best friend from his high school days; the members of his tennis team.

    Person A is probably ______________________________ .

    Person B's in-group members: his parents, but not his sister; his grandmother but not his grandfather; one of his uncles, but not the other two uncles. Another in-group consists of his best friend whom he met last year while skateboarding in the park; three of his classmates whom he met when he started classes a few months ago; two girls and a boy who live in his neighborhood.

    Person B is probably ______________________________ .

14. According to ¶ 12, why is it important for collectivists to maintain harmony?

    a) Because if there is a conflict, a group member might leave the group.
    b) Because if there is a conflict, everyone in the group will suffer until the conflict is resolved.

15. Which of these are **not** a teknonym? (¶ 12) (Circle all that apply.)

   a) The second daughter in our family is Anna, but everyone calls her ***ruti***, which means the second daughter in the family.

   b) The second daughter in my family is Anna, and everyone calls her Anna.

   c) My older brother's name is James, but we call him Jim.

   d) My oldest brother's name is James, but I call him ***destu*** which means my oldest brother.

16. Write ***individualist*** or ***collectivist*** after each description.

   a) I do what is best for me. ______________________

   b) I do what my in-group wants me to do. ______________________

   c) If my in-group is happy, then I'm happy. ______________________

   d) That man is my uncle; therefore, he is in my in-group. ________________

   e) That man is my uncle; however, he is not in my in-group. ______________

   f) My in-group wants me to change my hair-style, but I don't want to, so I won't. ______________________

17. Write one clarification question about a word, sentence, or idea that you do not understand in this unit. (If you understand everything, pretend that you don't.)

Part 2: Academic Vocabulary for Unit 3

Exercise 1: Words from context

Look at the paragraphs listed in the middle column of the chart below to find the words that have the meanings in the column on the right.

	Word	¶ *	Find the word that means . . .
1.		2	behave, or act, in a way that is similar to other people's group behavior
2.		4	an idea
3.		5	make something continue as it was in the past
4.		6	think about something carefully and make a judgment
5.		12	show

* **The symbol ¶ means paragraph number.** You can find the word in that paragraph.

Exercise 2: Vocabulary Fill-in Exercise

Choose the words in Exercise 1 above to fill in the blanks below.

1. After Tom had a car accident, he took his car to a repair shop and asked them to __________ the damage in order to help him decide whether he should fix it or buy a new one.
2. Yesterday, one of the students came to class without a shirt and with no shoes. His appearance did not __________________ to the rest of the class.
3. When you are driving a car, you should use your turn signals to __________________ when you are turning left or right.
4. Freedom of speech is an important _________________ in a democratic society.
5. After graduating from college, I wanted to ________________ a relationship with my former roommate, so we have continued to email each other.

Exercise 3: Applied Vocabulary

1. If all the students in a class are sitting in their seats and you want to ask the instructor a question, what do you do to indicate that you have a question?

2. Which of these are examples of someone trying to conform? (Choose all that apply.)
   a) The teacher tells us to use a black pen to write our essays, so I use a black pen.
   b) On my basketball team, everyone agreed to go to bed at 10:00 p.m. on the night before a game. However, I usually stay up until midnight.
   c) In my country, women are supposed to carry brightly-colored umbrellas, and men carry black ones. My sister often carries a black one.
   d) The law says that we should recycle plastics in a blue box and paper in a red box. I always do this.

3. If people want to maintain their health, what should they do? (Choose all that apply.)

   a) Exercise often.
   b) Sleep four hours a night.
   c) Smoke cigarettes.
   d) Eat balanced meals.

4. What is a good way to evaluate whether a college is a good one? (Choose one.)
   a) Find out if their basketball team has won any championships recently.
   b) Ask someone if you can get a part-time job there while you are a student.
   c) Talk to some people who graduated from the college in order to get their opinions.
   d) Research how much snow that area gets.

5. Do you understand these concepts clearly? Write *yes* or *no* in the blanks.
   a) norms ______
   b) in-groups ______
   c) technonyms ______
   d) attribution ______
   e) saving face ______

Part 3: Preparation for discussion for Unit 3

Think about your answers to these questions. You do not have to write your answers.

1. Do people in your country tend to stay in their hometowns most of their lives, or do many of them move away? Has your family stayed in the same hometown?

2. In ¶ 2, it talks about being excluded from a group and conforming to a group. Let's say that your in-group members decided to take a trip together, but you really didn't want to go. However, if you don't go, your in-group might exclude you in the future. Which would be worse for you: to be excluded from the group or be forced to conform to the group and go on the trip?

3. In ¶ 2, there is an example of the woman and the coat. Do you feel pressure in your country to wear certain clothes as this woman did?

4. In your hometown, are there a lot of jobs to choose from, or are people mainly farmers?

5. Who are the members of your most important in-group?

6. In ¶ 4, the tenth sentence says "norms, goals, and values shape the behavior of [the in-group's] members." Give me an example of how your in-group has shaped you.

7. Would you ask your in-group members questions like "How much money do you make?" or "What kind of sex life do you have?"

8. In your culture, are students expected to join many groups or just one? Did you join any clubs in high school?

9. In ¶ 10, it mentions calling a friend at 2:00 a.m. Would you think that it is strange to call a friend at 2:00 a.m. to talk about a problem?

10. Does your culture use teknonyms? Can you give an example?

11. In ¶ 13, the Greek secretary sounded rude on the phone because she thought the caller was a member of the out-group. Are people in your culture more polite to members of their in-group than out-group?

12. Do you agree with Dr. Chao that Dr. Douglas should have repaid the favor and hired Ms. Wang?

> ❖ For "Small-group Discussion" questions in the form of Students A, B, and C, see ***Supplementary Activities***, or download it free from www.ProLinguaAssociates.com.

> ❖ For "Whole-class Discussion" techniques and a suggested procedure, see the ***Supplementary Activities***, or download it free from www.prolinguaassociates.com.

> ❖ For "Applied Outside-class Interactions/Observations," see the ***Supplementary Activities***, or download it free from www.prolinguaassociates.com.

Part 4: A technique for writing good paraphrases

In most academic courses, students answer questions on tests and write papers that use information from a source. The source can be the course textbook, a newspaper, a magazine or an Internet article. One of the challenges for students is to show the instructor that they understand the source information, and they can do this by paraphrasing information, in other words, by explaining the information by using their own words and style. If a student just copies from the source, it doesn't show that they understood it. Even a child who doesn't understand information from a source can copy.

Exercise 1

Read the "Information from a source" below.

Information from a source

As mentioned above, norms are established by a group, and they specify how the group members should or should not behave. Interestingly, it's possible for the norms of a group to be different from the laws of a country. For example, there is a law against stealing in Italy. However, for cattle herders in Sardinia in Italy, the norm allows for stealing in certain situations. In their culture, equity is the norm. These cattle herders would explain their norm by saying, "God wants everyone to have the same; when someone has more, we take it away (i.e., steal) to do God's work" (Triandis, 1994a, 100). This has been the norm for many centuries even though Italian law, in fact, prohibits stealing.

Exercise 2

Which of these two paragraphs is a good paraphrase? Choose **A** or **B**.

A Norms are ways that people in a culture are expected to behave. However, sometimes, the norms and laws might be different. The author gives the example of cattle herders in Sardinia in Italy. This group of people believes that everyone is supposed to be treated equally, so this is their norm. As a result, if someone in the group has more than the others, it is acceptable for the others to steal from that person. In this case, the norm, stealing, is different from the law in Italy, in which stealing is illegal.

B Norms specify how group members should or should not behave. The author gives the example of cattle herders in Sardinia in Italy. Italian law prohibits stealing, but these herders' norm allows for stealing in certain situations because for them, equality is the norm. If someone has more, they take it away to do God's work.

Exercise 3

1) Read Unit 3.1, paragraph 1, about the reason for norms in collectivist cultures.
2) Without looking at that paragraph, fill in the blanks of this paraphrase with the words from the box.

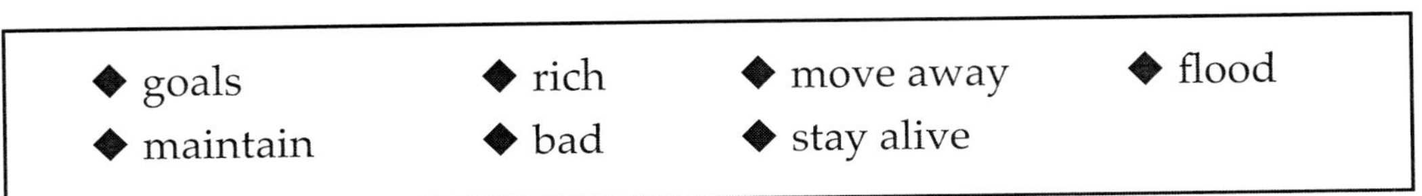

◆ goals	◆ rich	◆ move away	◆ flood
◆ maintain	◆ bad	◆ stay alive	

The authors explain the reasons why collectivist cultures have their norms. In these cultures, many of the people are farmers who are not very________________. When something ________________happens, for example a________________, all the people try to help each other. In other words, they depend on each other to ________________. The people have similar ____________, and they identify themselves a member of the group, not as individuals. Another important point is that these people tend to live in the same town all their lives because they are not rich enough to________________________. For this reason, they know their neighbors very well, and they try to get along with them. Interestingly, some collectivist societies are now rich, but they ________________ these norms.

Exercise 4

1) Choose one of these paragraphs:
   - ◆ Unit 3, paragraph 2
   - ◆ Unit 3, paragraph 3
2) Read the paragraph.
3) Write a paraphrase without looking at the paragraph while you are writing.
4) Re-read the paragraph in Unit 3.
5) Improve your paraphrase, if possible.

Part 5: Preview for Unit 4

Directions: Write your answers to these questions.

1. Let's say that you go to a coffee shop with three friends. Your friends order the same type of coffee. Would you tend to order the same type of coffee as they ordered, or would you tend to order a different type? ________________

2. When I am in my country . . . (Choose one.)

    a) I feel pressure to conform, so I try to conform to the norms.

    b) I feel pressure to conform, but I often do not conform to the norms.

    c) I don't feel pressure to conform, but I usually conform to the norms.

    d) I don't feel pressure to conform, and I often do not conform to the norms.

Unit 4

Conformity: Advantages of fitting in

Reading

[1] Kim and Markus (1999) introduce their article about conformity with this example. A woman at a coffee shop in the U.S. feels good about ordering an unusual drink, for example, a decaffeinated cappuccino with nonfat milk, because it's not what most people order. She feels that it's her right to order the drink exactly the way that she wants it, and the waiter brings it to her without any comment. The best taste is the one that she, herself, likes. However, if a woman in an East Asian country orders a drink, she hesitates to order an unusual drink that no one else is ordering. Other people in the shop are likely to think that she is a difficult person who expects others to do things her way. As a result, she might decide that it is not proper for her to expect this coffee shop to make an unusual drink just for her. It will not feel right to drink a decaffeinated cappuccino with nonfat milk in that context, meaning in her culture. The best-tasting coffee is the one that "normal" people drink. A type of drink that people don't traditionally order will not taste "right."

[2] Individualists often assume that collectivists are conforming to the norms because they feel pressure from their society; however, this is an incorrect assumption. They are conforming because it gives them a sense of connection to their group members. Acting like others feels good, and this gives them a feeling of satisfaction. An example of this is shown in an experiment that researchers conducted using puzzles with Asian and American children. In some situations, the children chose their own puzzle, and in others, their in-group members chose the puzzle. The Asian children tended to work longer than the American children on the puzzles that were chosen by their group members (Iyengar and Lepper, 1999).

[3] Collectivists have a fear of being separated from the group or of doing things alone. Thus, they are willing to avoid expressing their own individual opinion if they don't agree with the group. As a result, they are able to maintain harmony, which is highly valued. This is reinforced by the fact that parents and schools teach children that it is very important to obey their elders, respect traditions, and follow the social norms. As a result, people have a sense of satisfaction when they are doing what the norms tell them to do. If someone tries to be independent or to stand out in any way, they are considered to be immature, and their behavior is seen as unnatural. Therefore, conformity is emphasized.

[4] In contrast to the importance that collectivists put on conformity, individualists, who value freedom and autonomy, tend to view conformity negatively. From the time that individualists are young, they are told that they are responsible for what happens

to themselves and that they need to make their own choices without letting other people pressure them. Individualists feel that if someone conforms, the reason is usually because they are responding to group pressure, and this shows a lack of personal creativity and autonomy. The idea that someone would willingly conform in order to maintain group harmony is inconceivable to individualists. If someone is conforming, individualists become concerned that other people are controlling that person. In sum, individualists feel that it is important to try to be unique although the degree of uniqueness depends on the situation (Kim and Markus, 1999).

5 Researchers conducted a study concerning the collectivists' desire to fit in and the individualists' desire to be unique. The research involved 29 Asians and 27 Americans. Researchers approached a person (a "responder") who was alone and asked them to fill out a questionnaire and told them that they would receive a free pen as a gift. (The questions on the questionnaire were, in fact, not important in this experiment.) After each responder had filled out the questionnaire, the researcher showed the responder five pens; a minority of the pens (i.e., one or two of the five pens) were one color (e.g., orange) and the majority (i.e., three or four pens) were a different color (e.g., green). The majority and minority colors were occasionally reversed so that the majority color was sometimes orange and sometimes green. The Asians tended to choose the majority color, while the Americans tended to choose the minority color. Interestingly, the reason why the Asians chose the majority was not because they liked the color of the pen, but rather because they were attracted to the "suggestion of a group" of the majority color. Similarly, the Americans preferred the minority color as it suggested "separateness" (Kim and Markus, 1999).

6 This does not mean that individualists never conform to a group and that collectivists always conform. In a famous study, Solomon Asch, asked participants ("subjects") to take part in a "vision (eyesight) test." Actually, the experiment was not about vision but rather about conformity. Asch invited the subjects in groups of five to come into a room. Four of the subjects were secretly working for Asch. In experiments like this one, these secret workers are called "confederates," and they are privately told what to do before an experiment begins. The other subject (the true subject) really thought that the experiment was about eyesight. In the room, Asch showed the group a pair of charts. In Chart 1, there was a vertical line. In Chart 2, there were three vertical lines (Lines A, B, and C), one of which matched the length of the line in Chart 1, and the other two lines were clearly of different lengths. The five subjects were told to identify the line in Chart 2 which was the same length as the one in Chart 1. The confederates always gave their choice first, and sometimes they chose the correct line. However, at other times, the confederates purposely chose the wrong line; for example, if the matching line in Chart 2 was Line C,

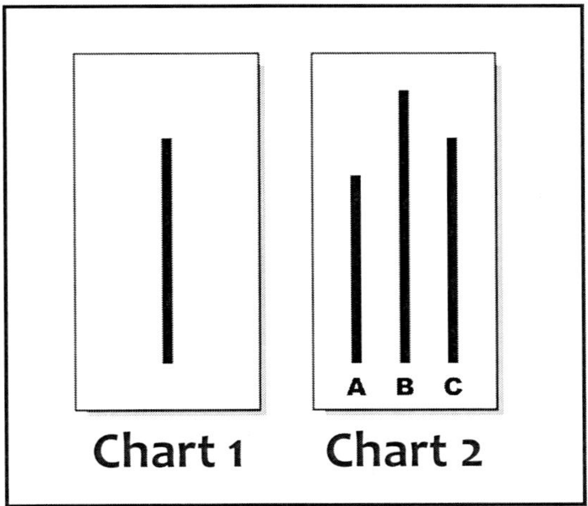

all the confederates said Line A was the matching line. After the confederates gave their answer, the true subject answered. Asch wanted to see whether the true subject would conform to the "incorrect" answer that the confederates gave, or whether the true subject would give the correct answer.

7 When Asch conducted this experiment with American subjects, he found that true subjects gave the incorrect answer about a third of the time. What is even more surprising is that almost 75% of these true subjects gave the incorrect answer at least once. In other words, a large majority of these subjects from an individualist country conformed to the group at least once (Asch, 1956). When the subjects were interviewed after the experiment, most of them said that they knew their answer was incorrect, but they felt that they wanted to conform to the group (Simons, et. al., 1987).

8 When a researcher conducted the Asch experiment with Japanese subjects, he expected that more of the true subjects would agree with the confederates since there seems to be a greater tendency for conformity in Japan, a collectivist country. However, interestingly, the true Japanese subjects gave the incorrect answer only 20% of the time. In fact, the Japanese actually showed anti-conformity tendencies! When the four confederates chose the correct line, 34% of the Japanese subjects chose the wrong line (Fragler, 1970). The reason for this could be because the confederates were not members of the Japanese subjects' in-group. Collectivists tend to conform to their in-groups but are less willing to do so with out-group members. The fact that 34% of the Japanese subjects made anti-conformity choices could indicate that they were resisting pressure from the others in the group, who were strangers—and thus, were out-group members (Carson and Nelson 1994). On the other hand, individualists are apt to be less sensitive to the difference between in-groups and out-groups, and therefore would be more likely to conform with strangers than a collectivist would.

Part 1: Study guide for Unit 4

1. According to the story about the coffee drinkers in ¶ 1, the woman in the U.S. ordered a decaffeinated cappuccino with nonfat milk because ___. (Choose all that are correct.)
   a) it is unique
   b) it is popular
   c) it tastes good
   d) she doesn't want to appear different from other people

2. According to the story about the coffee drinkers in ¶ 1, the woman in East Asia probably would not order a decaffeinated cappuccino with nonfat milk because ___. (Choose all that are correct.)
   a) she would feel that it would not taste good
   b) people around her might get a negative impression of her
   c) the coffee shop would not know how to make it
   d) she feels pressure not to order it even though she might really like it

3. True or false? According to ¶ 2, most individualists understand correctly the reason why collectivists conform. ____________________

4. Paragraphs 2-4 discuss conforming. Choose the words from the box to fill in the chart below about collectivists' and individualists' attitudes about conforming.

◆ are taught to be independent	◆ believe that it maintains group harmony
◆ think non-conforming is abnormal	◆ consider being unique as a good thing
◆ feel connected to others	◆ prefer freedom to make their own choice
◆ don't like group pressure	◆ feel good when conforming

Collectivists' attitudes about conforming	*Individualists' attitudes about conforming*

5. The "puzzle" story in ¶ 2 demonstrates that Asian children ____ .

    a) feel pleasure when they are conforming

    b) prefer the freedom to make their own choice

    c) are pressured to conform to others

    d) are similar to American children

6. The following is a paraphrase of ¶ 5. There are seven mistakes underlined in the content, including "conform." Correct the mistakes by changing words and phrases.

    1) The study was about individuals' preference to conform and collectivists' preference to be unique. 2) After answering questions on a questionnaire, they were shown six pens and were allowed to choose several. 3) They could choose among three colors. 4) One color was the majority of the pens, and the other was a minority of them. 5) The Americans tended to choose one that was in the minority, and the Asians chose one that was in the minority. 6) Their decisions were influenced by how much they liked the color.

Questions 7-10 are about the study in ¶ 6.

7. The confederates
    a) thought that the experiment was about vision
    b) knew that the experiment was about conformity

8. When they saw the two charts, the confederates ____ .
    a) purposely conformed to each other even when they knew that the answer was incorrect
    b) purposely tried not to conform to each other even when they knew that their answer was incorrect

9. The true subjects ____ .
    a) thought that the experiment was about vision
    b) knew that the experiment was about conformity

10. When they saw the two charts, the true subjects chose the wrong answer___.
    a) by mistake. They really did not know which line was the matching one
    b) because the other members had chosen that line, even though they really knew that that line was not the matching line

11. According to ¶ 7-8, who conformed more in these experiments: Americans or Japanese? ______________________

12. According to ¶ 8, what is an anti-conformity tendency?
    a) The confederates chose the wrong line, so the subjects also chose the wrong line.
    b) The confederates chose the wrong line, but the subjects chose the correct line.
    c) The confederates chose the correct line, but the subjects chose the wrong line.
    d) The confederates chose the correct line, so the subjects also chose the correct line.

13. Write one clarification question about a word, sentence, or idea that you do not understand in this unit. (If you understand everything, pretend that you don't.)

Part 2: Academic Vocabulary for Unit 4

Exercise 1: Words from context

Look at the paragraphs listed in the middle column of the chart below to find the words that have the meanings in the column on the right.

	Word	¶ *	Find the word that means . . .
1.	heisitate	1	Waits or pauses a moment before doing something
2.	inmature	3	not adult-like in behavior or actions
3.	emphasize	3	showed that an idea or opinion is especially important
4.	Autonomy	4	the ability or freedom to make your own decisions without anyone trying to control you
5.	Inconceivable	4	too strange or unusual to be possible or real

* **The symbol ¶ means paragraph number.** You can find the word in that paragraph.

Exercise 2: Vocabulary Fill-in Exercise

Choose the words in Exercise 1 above to fill in the blanks below.

1. Twenty years ago, it was ____________________ that people would be able to take pictures with their phones.

2. When Ben asks Sue for a date, she sometimes ____________________ before saying that she will go out with him. Now, he is wondering if she doesn't really want to have a date with him.

3. At my job, I can decide what time I want to come to work and what time I want to leave. In fact, if I want to, I don't have to come to work; I can work from home by using the Internet. In other words, I have a lot of ________________.

4. Even though my brother is in college, he acts like a junior high school student. In a word, he is very ________________.

5. At a meeting about children's health, specialists ________________________ the importance of breakfast.

Exercise 3: Applied Vocabulary

1. When you were a child, what good study habits were emphasized by adults in your life?

2. When you were in high school, did your parents give you a lot of autonomy? _____
If you had children, would you give them more or less autonomy than you had? _____
Explain.

3. In which of these situations would you hesitate before accepting or rejecting the offer?
   a) A classmate who usually sits next to you asks, "Would you like a piece of candy?"
   b) Your parents ask you, "Would you like us to give you $1,000?"
   c) Your teacher asks you, "Would like to go to a party tonight at my home?"
   d) Your friend asks you, "Could you call me tonight at 2:00 a.m.?"

4. Choose the things that seem inconceivable to you.
___ There will be no more wars in the world.
___ I will live in a foreign country for most of my life.
___ I will get married.
___ I will be rich enough to own several homes.
___ I will have a lot of children.
___ I will retire from work before I am 50 years old.
___ I will be a performer in a movie.
___ (Write one more thing about your future that is inconceivable to you.)
____

5. Do you know anyone who acts immature? ______ Describe what that person does.

Part 3: Preparation for discussion for Unit 4

Think about your answers to these questions. You do not have to write your answers.

1. When you are in your country, would you avoid ordering a type of drink because people might think that you are hard to get along with?

2. Did your parents teach you that it was very important to obey your elders, respect traditions and follow social norms? Can you give an example of how they taught you these?

3. Let's say that your classmate dresses differently from the others, has an unusual hairstyle, and eats unusual food for lunch. Would you think that this person is immature and unnatural, or would you think that they are interesting (in other words, have a positive feeling about them)? Explain.

4. According to the Asch experiment, 33% of the time, subjects gave the wrong answer in order to conform to the group. Do you think that this is bad for society or is it good? Explain.

5. Do you think that you tend to make conformity or anti-conformity choices when you are in your country?

❖ For "Small-group Discussion" questions in the form of Students A, B, and C, see *Supplementary Activities*, or download it free from www.ProLinguaAssociates.com.

❖ For "Whole-class Discussion" techniques and a suggested procedure, see the *Supplementary Activities*, or download it free from www.prolinguaassociates.com.

❖ For "Applied Outside-class Interactions/Observations," see the *Supplementary Activities*, or download it free from www.prolinguaassociates.com.

Part 4: A technique for writing good answers on tests

Refer to a source.

As mentioned in Unit 3, it is common for students to use information from a source in academic papers. In this unit, you will practice using some expressions to introduce the source that you are using. This technique will help your instructor know which information is your own and which comes from a source. Also, these expressions are useful in academic writing.

Exercise 1

1) Read the Information from the Source 1 below.
2) Read the Sample Test Question under the Source.
3) Read the student's answer. Fill in the blanks using the phrases from the smaller box.

Information from Source 1

In Japan, people are expected to control normal emotions . . . in an experiment . . . Americans and Japanese were shown a movie of someone's hand being cut. The subjects of the experiment were shown the movie under two conditions: alone and in the presence of others. The Americans and Japanese expressed the same emotions in the 'alone' condition, but the Japanese expressed less emotions in the 'presence of others condition' (Triandis, 1994b, p. 34).

Sample Test Question 1

Many Asians seem to not show their emotions. Is this because they don't feel the same emotions as non-Asians?

- ◆ From the study, we learn that
- ◆ The results from a study showed

Student's answer

____________________________that Asians feel the same emotions as other people, but they have different norms for expressing them. ____________________________ when they are shown a movie of someone's hand being cut, Japanese who were alone showed the same pained expression on their faces as Americans did. In other words, they felt the same emotion. However, when other people were in the room while the Japanese were watching the movie, they showed less emotion on their faces than the Americans did.

Exercise 2

1) Read the Information from the Source below.

2) Read the Sample Test Question under the Source.

3) Read the student's answer. Fill in the blanks using the phrases from the smaller box.

Information from Source 2

A recent study looked at how a "considerate" office supervisor should behave. The subjects of the study, who were in Hong Kong and Great Britain, were given a hypothetical situation: A co-worker was having personal problems. What should the supervisor do? In Hong Kong, the subjects of the study said that the supervisor should meet with just the other workers to discuss the problem, in other words, when the worker who was having the problem was not present. That is what a considerate supervisor would do. In Britain, they said that it would be very inconsiderate for the supervisor to discuss in public the co-worker's problem (Smith & Bond, 1994).

Sample Test Question 2

What is the best way to help a co-worker who is having a problem?

- ◆ According to researchers,
- ◆ according to the findings of the study

Student's answer

The method of helping a co-worker with a problem depends on the location of the company. ______________________________, the best way to help the co-worker in Hong Kong would be for the supervisor and other workers to discuss the problem in the absence of the co-worker who was having the problem. However, ______________________________ in Great Britain, that approach would be inconsiderate.

Expressions for Referring to a Source

- ◆ According to the results of the study, …
- ◆ According to the findings of the study, …
- ◆ According to researchers, …
- ◆ According to experts, …
- ◆ According to the text, …
- ◆ From the research, we learned that …
- ◆ From the studies, we discovered that …
- ◆ The authors explained that …

Exercise 3: Answer the Sample Test Questions below. Use Expressions for Referring to a Source in the box above.

Sample Test Question 1

In Unit 2, paragraph 14, it talks about Korean and American skiers. Do Koreans and Americans like to ski in groups? Explain how your answer is connected to individualism and collectivism.

Sample Test Question 2

In Unit 4, paragraph 5, we read about the desire to fit in or to be unique. Who showed a stronger desire to fit in, and who showed a stronger desire to be unique: Asians or Americans? Explain your answer.

Part 5: Preview for Unit 5

Directions: Write your answers to these questions.

1. In your culture, are there special colors for men and special colors for women? For example, are there colors of cars or umbrellas that men should choose and different colors that women should choose?

2. Do you think that the large cities in your country are safe or dangerous?

3. When you were a high school student, did your school have strict rules about what students could wear, the style and color of their hair, and girls' make up?

Questions 4 and 5: Read the situation below and then answer the questions.

Situation

You are the president of a company. You have two workers (Worker A and Worker B) who worked on a project.

- **Worker A** worked the hardest and did excellent work. He is well off financially. (In other words, he is not poor).
- **Worker B** did not work as hard as A, but his work was okay. He is poor; he has a lot of medical bills because his daughter is ill.

Question 4

At the end of the project, there is an extra $400 that you can give to the workers. Who would you give the money to?

a) I would give the $400 to Worker A, who worked harder and is rich.
b) I would give $200 to each of them.
c) I would give the $400 to Worker B, who is poor and has medical expenses.

Question 5

At the end of the project, you find that the project lost $400, and you must take the money from the workers' salary. Who will you take the money from?

a) I would take the $400 from Worker A, who worked harder and is rich.
b) I would take $200 from each of them.
c) I would take the $400 from Worker B, who is poor and has medical expenses.

Unit 5

5.1 Tight and loose cultures:

advantages and disadvantages of strict rules of behavior

Reading

1 An American husband and wife were teaching English in Asia. One rainy day, both were carrying black umbrellas as they were walking to school. Along the way, they met some of their students, who had big smiles on their faces and were chuckling. When asked why they were laughing, the students said that it was funny to see a woman carrying a black umbrella; in their country, women are supposed to carry umbrellas that are red (or some other bright color).

2 A number of Asian countries are considered to have **tight cultures**, in which society expects people to behave according to specific norms. If someone deviates from a norm, they can be criticized or even punished. An example of this happened in one tight Asian country. One day a high school student arrived at class two minutes late, and as she was about to enter the room, the teacher (who was angry at the student's lateness) slammed the door on her head and killed her. A considerable number of people criticized the teacher and said that he must have been mentally unstable. However, some newspaper writers said that although it was a tragedy that the student was killed, they could understand the teacher's situation because he was trying to set an example for all the students in his class that it is necessary to be on time, an important norm in that culture. (Triandis, 1994b)

[3] In **loose cultures**, e.g., Canada and the United States, few students would have been punished at all for missing the start of class by just two minutes, because deviations from the norms on punctuality are tolerated. On the other hand, in tight cultures, people put a strong emphasis on the value of norms, and everyone is expected to follow them.

[4] One characteristic of loose cultures is that they are often heterogeneous, which means that there are a lot of variations among people. Because of the large variety of customs in heterogeneous cultures, it's difficult for people to agree on what specific norms people should follow. Another characteristic is that loose cultures are often located between other distinct, larger cultures. For example, Thailand, a loose culture, is between India and China, which are considered tight. Also, we can find that cultures that have a low population density (e.g., ones in a desert) are often loose. Triandis (1994) compares this to traffic and driving regulations. If there are many cars on a road, it's important for everyone to follow the rule of driving on the correct side of the road. However, if there is only one car on the road, it is possible to drive on either side of the road without causing any problems.

[5] Tight cultures have their own unique characteristics. They tend to be homogeneous; in them, people are quite similar to each other, and because of this, they tend to agree about what the norms should be. In contrast to loose cultures, which were described above, tight cultures are apt to have a high population density. In addition, cultures which require people to coordinate with each other in order to survive, e.g., agricultural societies, are often tight.

[6] When we compare tight and loose cultures, we find differences between them concerning social well-being and quality of life. In tight cultures, norms are clearly defined, and if people follow those norms and behave as everyone else does, they can avoid criticism. They know what they are supposed to do in every situation. There seem to be some benefits to this. Singapore, Hong Kong, and Tokyo are some of the safest cities in the world, whereas in New York, whose population is similar in size to those other cities, the homicide rate is much higher. Also, it is believed that the quality of manufactured products is better in tight cultures. However, there seems to be a drawback to the tight societies. Because there tends to be greater control of people's lives, there could be more suicides (Triandis, 1994b).

[7] As mentioned above, an example of a loose culture is Thailand. Triandis (1994) illustrates the characteristics of this loose culture. In Thailand, an employee might become bored with their work or decide to take a vacation and just leave their job without saying anything to anyone. If they are absent from work for a certain length of time, their employer will understand that the employee has quit. In contrast, in a tight culture, if workers decided to quit their job, they would be expected to notify their employer in advance.

[8] It is sometimes difficult for people to adjust to their home culture after returning from an extended stay in any other culture. This can be especially true for someone from a tight culture who returns home after living in a loose culture—and vice versa.

[9] An Asian student described her experience of returning to her native country after spending time in the U.S. She said, "[In the U.S.] I had a perm in my hair but the school [at home] had a rule which said no permanents, so my teacher told me I had to cut off the curls, and I did. Also, my hair had become a lighter color in the U.S. because I had spent more time in the sun in the U.S., but my teacher said I had to dye my hair black. Also, my classmates teased me, too, about my lighter-colored hair. So I was unhappy. I didn't want to dye it black because I explained, 'This is my natural hair'" (Kidder, 1992, 385).

[10] In some schools in tight cultures, students whose natural hair color is lighter than others can be required to darken their hair. This rule applies to even students who have never lived abroad. The school officials feel that hair color is an important aspect of a proper appearance—as important as shirts, pants, skirts, and shoes. Some schools even have rules concerning the color of students' underwear.

[11] One student arrived home from the U.S., and the first thing her mother did was check to make sure that she was not wearing make-up and had not pierced her ears.

[12] In another case, a Japanese girl realized that her style of walking had changed during her life in America. She started pointing her toes outward when she walked, and her steps were bigger. When she returned to Japan, she had to relearn how to walk in a way that was closer to the norm for females in her country—with toes pointed in and with smaller steps.

[13] Other students mentioned that, during their stay in a loose culture, they had developed the custom of looking at people directly in the eyes and of smiling at strangers. They also began directly expressing their opinions while abroad. When they returned home, they felt a need to change these habits.

14 People from loose cultures can have similar experiences when returning from life in a tight culture. A teacher from the U.S. enjoyed the sense of security she had while living in an Asian city because of the low crime rate. She had become accustomed to taking the subway anywhere in the city, even late at night, without any worry for her safety. Upon returning to her home in Chicago, she felt a loss of freedom because she had to avoid going to certain areas, especially at night, because it was risky (Kidder, 1992).

5.2 Distributing money:
need vs. merit

15 A study was done in India and the United States that included university students from both countries. The students were presented with stories about twelve companies; half of the companies had had a successful year, so they had a positive distribution (i.e., extra money to share among some of the workers), and the other half of the companies had not made much money, so they had a negative distribution (i.e., a pay-cut that some—or all—of the workers would get) due to business problems. The stories also included two types of workers in each company: an excellent one who was financially comfortable and an average worker who had a poor financial situation at home and also had a family member who was ill. First, the students had to decide how, for a successful company, they would distribute resources (a positive distribution of a $200 bonus). And there were five possible ways that they could do this: Option 1: give the entire bonus of $200 to the average-working, needy person, and give none to the hard-working, richer worker; Option 2: give $150 to the needy worker, and $50 to the hard-working one; Option 3: $100 to both; Option 4: $50 to the needy worker, and $150 to the hard-working one; Option 5: none to the needy person and all $200 to the hard-working one.

16 Next, they also had to decide how they would manage a negative distribution of a $200 pay-cut for a company that was in financial trouble. Likewise, for this situation as well, there were five possible ways that they could do this. For example, take no money from the average-working, needy person and take the $200 pay-cut from the excellent one who was financially comfortable, etc.

17 The researchers divided the results into the following three categories. If the Indian and/or American students chose Options #1 or #2, it was considered a "need" decision. Option #3 was an "equality" decision, and Options #4 and #5 were considered "merit" decisions. They found that when there was a bonus to distribute, for the American respondents, "merit" was the most popular decision (49% for merit compared to 16% for "need"), while the Indian students' results were almost the exact opposite. Among the Indian students, 52% chose "need" as the preferable decision, compared to only 16% who chose "merit." In deciding how to distribute the negative resources (the pay-cut), both nationalities thought that the needy worker should not get their pay cut; 65% of the Indians and 41% of the Americans favored this option (Segall et al, 1999).

18 The results suggest that from the perspective of Indians, who are collectivists, the person who is in need should receive the best treatment (either by getting a bonus or by not getting a pay-cut). However, when there is extra money, the Americans (individualists) prefer to give a reward to those who deserve it, thanks to their hard work (rather than reward those who need money), but they do not want to worsen the situation of a needy person when money must be taken away (Segall et al, 1999). Researchers conducted a similar study that compared Koreans (collectivists) and Americans, in which the Koreans had results that were similar to those of the Indians (Leung and Park, 1986).

19 Researchers conducted a similar experiment with Chinese and American subjects. In this study, the subjects were asked to imagine that they had co-workers, and some co-workers were needy but not good workers, while other co-workers were financially comfortable and good workers. On top of that, sometimes the imaginary co-workers were in-group members, and sometimes they were out-group members. The results indicated that, to the Chinese, it mattered whether the imaginary co-workers were members of their in-group or out-group. If the co-workers were in their in-group, then the Chinese were more likely to show sympathy toward a needy one. On the other hand, if the Chinese imagined that the co-worker was an out-group member, then they preferred to allocate the money based on merit. In contrast, for the Americans, the fact that an imaginary co-worker was an in-group or out-group member didn't matter very much (Segall, et al., 1991).

20 How participants in the research studies that are described above decide what is fair depends on the goal. If the goal is to preserve harmony and group unity (a common collectivist goal), then equality or need seems to be preferable. Collectivists explain their decision to divide a reward equally (by giving a needy co-worker more money than they deserve) by saying that it is important for the group to function smoothly because, in this way, they will be able to accomplish more together as a group than they could as individuals. If one person gets more, then it might cause jealousy and disrupt the group's

ability to perform. On the other hand, if the goal is to reward individual excellence (a common individualist goal), then merit seems to be the fairest way to distribute a reward. Individualists feel that the person who worked the hardest deserves the most reward because if they don't get it, they may not want to work as hard on the next project.

21 This focus on rewarding individuals in individualist cultures and preserving harmony and group unity in collectivist ones has had an interesting impact on the societies. According to research, individualism tends to be associated with higher levels of economic growth (Hafstede, 1980). In individualist countries, where people are rewarded according to their merit, there tends to be greater incentive to be innovative, which can lead to a wealthier society. However, because there is more competition among individuals for rewards, we find more social problems with crime, suicide, divorce, stress and mental illness than in collectivist cultures.

22 In collectivist cultures, on the other hand, people have a stronger system of social support (i.e., help that is available from family and friends); this can result in better health. Studies show that people with high levels of social support are more likely to stop smoking and lose weight (Janis, 1983). Also, because there tends to be less competition in collectivist cultures, there seems to be less stress in daily life. Nevertheless, there is one kind of stress which collectivists are exposed to: the trauma that they experience when one of their in-group members suffers from a problem. Individualists, on the other hand, tend to be less emotionally attached to others, so generally speaking, they experience less stress when a group member has a problem (Triandis et al, 1988).

Part 1: Study guide for Unit 5

1. According to ¶ 1, the example about the red and black umbrellas shows that Japan tends to be __a__ .
   a) a tight culture b) a loose culture

2. In Unit 4, ¶ 1, there are stories about ordering decaffeinated cappuccino coffee. From the story that happened in the East Asian country, we could say that this Asian country tends to be __a__.
   a) a tight culture b) a loose culture

3. Look at Unit 5, ¶ 3-6 and fill in the chart using the words from the box.

homogeneous	more suicides	deviation is allowed
e.g., Thailand	more crime	better products
deviation is not allowed	e.g., China	heterogeneous
lower population density	safer	found between larger cultures

Tight Cultures	Loose Cultures
homogeneous	deviation is allowed
more suicides	e.g. Thailand
Better products	more crime
e.g china	he
Deviation is not allowed	
safer	

4. In the "hair-perm" example in ¶ 9, the student who got a perm __b__.
   a) followed the norms of her culture b) deviated from the norms of her culture

Questions 5-7 are about ¶ 14-18.

5. In the blanks, write ***merit decision, need decision,*** or ***equality decision***.
   a) The reward should be divided between both workers equally. __equa__
   b) The excellent worker should get the reward. __me__
   c) The average, poor worker should get the reward. __need__
   d) The excellent worker should not get a pay-cut. __merit__
   e) The average, poor worker should not get a pay-cut. __need__
   f) The pay-cut should be taken from both workers' salaries. __equality__

6. Fill in the chart about the study of "merit vs. need" in ¶ 17.

Gets bonus	Person with need	Person with merit
Who should get the bonus? *(Indians said)*	57 %	16 %
Who should get the bonus? *(Americans said)*	16 %	49 %
Not get a pay-cut		
Who should not get the paycut? *(Indians said)*	65 %	
Who should not get the paycut? *(Americans said)*	41 %	

7. What would excellent individualist workers probably do if they were not rewarded more than the average worker? (Choose all that apply.)
   a) They would not complain because they would want to maintain harmony in the group.
   b) They would leave the group and join a new one that would reward them.
   c) They would work harder on the next project so that the group could succeed.
   d) They might not work as hard on the project.

8. Match the words on the left to the definitions on the right from ¶ 21.

c economic growth	a) creative
d incentive	b) sickness of the mind, e.g., depression
a innovative	c) increase in money or value
e impact	d) motivation
b mental illness	e) effect

9. This question refers to ¶ 21-22. There are some advantages and disadvantages to individualist societies that reward merit and to collectivist societies that do not reward merit. What are they?
   a) Advantages to individualist societies for rewarding merit: ____________________
   ____
   b) Disadvantages to individualist societies for rewarding merit: ____________________
   ____
   c) Advantages to collectivist societies for not rewarding merit: ____________________
   ____
   d) Disadvantages to collectivist societies for not rewarding merit: ____________________
   ____

10. Write one clarification question about a word, sentence, or idea that you do not understand in this unit. (If you understand everything, pretend that you don't.)

Part 2: Academic Vocabulary for Unit 5

Exercise 1: Words from context

Look at the paragraphs listed in the middle column of the chart below to find the words that have the meanings on the right.

	Word	¶ *	Find the word that means . . .
1.	unstable	2	likely to change suddenly, usually to a worse condition
2.	distinct	4	clearly different
3.	adjust	8	make changes that are necessary in a new situation
4.	impact	21	effect; influence
5.	incentive	21	a situation, or reward, that encourages you to work harder

* **The symbol "¶" means paragraph.** You can find the word in that paragraph.

Exercise 2: Vocabulary Fill-in Exercise

Choose the words in Exercise 1 above to fill in the blanks below.

1. Even though French and English share some similar words, they are distinct languages.
2. My mother is a lawyer, and this had an impact on my decision to study law.
3. To make enough money to buy a new car was Dan's unstable for getting a part-time job.
4. Mari decided to quit her job and find a new one because of the incentive economic situation of the company that she had been working for.
5. When we talk to someone who does not know our language very well, we need to adjust how fast we speak.

Exercise 3: Applied Vocabulary

1. Choose one of the questions and answer it.
   - If you are living in a foreign country now, what has been a situation that you had to adjust to?
   - When you bought your most recent computer, what did you have to adjust in order to make it better?
   - If you have a roommate, how did you adjust in order to get along with that person?

2. What is the incentive that makes you study hard in school?

3. Who do you think had the greatest impact on what you like to do: your mother, father, a relative, a friend, or a teacher?

4. In this class, is there someone who has a distinct characteristic, for example, a way of talking, a hairstyle, a tattoo, a type of clothing, or a habit? Explain.

5. Think about your life. Tell about a time when your life seemed unstable.

Part 3: Preparation for discussion for Unit 5

Think about your answers to these questions. You do not have to write your answers.

1. Does your culture have a norm about special colors for males, and other colors for females?
2. Is your culture tight or loose? Give some examples.
3. Do you like living in a tight or loose culture?
4. In the study about the $200-bonus distribution, some people felt that it should be distributed equally to all the workers, some said that more should be given to the workers who needed it the most, and others said that it should be given to the hardest workers. Who do you think that it should be given to? Explain.
5. In the study about the negative distribution, some people felt that all the workers should get their pay cut, some people felt that the workers who needed the money the most should not have their pay cut, and some people felt that the hardest workers should not get their pay cut. Who do you agree with? Explain.
6. Do you think that there is more stress in your country, or in other countries? Explain.
7. When you are in your country, do you feel like you have good social support? Explain.
8. When one of your in-group members has a problem, does it cause you yourself a lot of stress? Explain.

❖ For "Small-group Discussion" questions in the form of Students A, B, and C, see *Supplementary Activities*, or download it free from www.ProLinguaAssociates.com.

❖ For "Whole-class Discussion" techniques and a suggested procedure, see the *Supplementary Activities*, or download it free from www.prolinguaassociates.com.

❖ For "Applied Outside-class Interactions/Observations," see the *Supplementary Activities*, or download it free from www.prolinguaassociates.com.

Part 4: A technique for writing good answers on tests

Impress your instructor by explaining something that was interesting to you.

These are comments that you should not say to your teacher:

◆ "This is boring." ◆ "I don't like this textbook." ◆ "This is too hard."

Students in elementary school sometimes make comments like these to their teachers, and it does not impress them!

This is a technique that will impress your teachers. All teachers think that their subjects are interesting. In fact, many of them think that their subject is the most interesting one in the world. For example, history teachers probably think that history is extremely interesting and important for everyone. Therefore, if you can find some interesting information about your teachers' subjects, you will probably impress them.

On a quiz or in an essay, you can use the expressions in the box below to introduce an idea that you thought was interesting.

Expressions

- Interestingly, …
- It is interesting that …
- I found it interesting that …
- What is interesting about this is (that) …

Exercise 1

Read the "Information from a source" in the box below.

Information from a source

In cultures that are considered "tight cultures," people are expected to strictly follow the norms of society. Anyone who does not may be criticized, or even punished, by others. In this kind of culture, the norm is for high school students to arrive a little early for class and to never be late. It was reported in a newspaper that "a teacher slammed a heavy door on the head of a student who was two minutes late for class, [which killed] her." While most of the commentaries in the newspaper expressed horror at the incident, some writers said that they could understand the teacher's actions since he "was trying to teach the students to be on time—a very important value" in this society. (Triandis, 1994b, p. 159)

Exercise 2

[1] Read the Sample Test Question 1 and Student A's answer below.
[2] Fill in the blanks with words from the box.

- ◆ start on time and
- ◆ follow the norm
- ◆ which can interrupt
- ◆ What is interesting about

Sample Test Question 1: Why did the teacher kill the student?

Student A's answer

The reason why the teacher killed the student was because she didn't ______________ of society. The norm was to arrive early for class, but she was late. In this culture, people like this student, who don't follow the norms, may be punished. ____________ ______________________ this situation is that the student was only two minutes late. It is probably rare for students to ever be late. As a result, classes in this country probably __________________________ students learn more. In some countries which are not tight, students might be late, ____ the lesson for all the other students.

Exercise 3

[1] Read the Sample Test Question 2 and Student A's answer below.
[2] Fill in the blanks with words from the box.

Sample Test Question 2

Look at the story about the hotel reservation in Unit 1, paragraphs 1-2, of this book. Why did the Indian clerk put an X on the "wrong line"?

- ◆ unaware of the confusion
- ◆ is interesting that
- ◆ the wrong line

Student A's answer

In the story about the hotel reservation in India, the Indian clerk did not put an "X" on ______________________________. For his culture, he completed the form correctly. It ______________________________ the clerk worked for the only Western-style hotel in Mysore. He probably had contact with many foreigners, yet he was ______________________________ that the forms probably caused.

Exercise 4

1) Choose three of the Sample Test Questions under the box.
2) For each question, first, answer it in your own words.
3) **After** you answer a question, tell what was interesting. Include one of the expressions in the box below.

Expressions

- Interestingly, ...
- It is interesting that ...
- I found it interesting that ...
- What is interesting about this is (that) ...

Sample Test Question 1: In Unit 1, ¶ 9, why do some men have more than one wife?

Sample Test Question 2: In the study in Unit 2, ¶ 2-4, who shared their food more: the Asian or the American children?

Sample Test Question 3: In Unit 3, ¶ 7, do Americans tend to belong to many clubs or only a few clubs?

Sample Test Question 4: In Unit 3, ¶ 12, what are "teknonyms"?

Sample Test Question 5: In Unit 4, ¶ 8, how many Japanese chose the anti-conformity choices?

Part 5: Preview for Unit 6

Directions: Write your answers to these questions.

1. If you go to a party, but you know very few of the other guests, how do you feel?

   a) I feel excited because it is a chance for me to meet some new people.
   b) I feel shy because I don't know what to say to people whom I don't know.

2. When was the most recent time that you complimented someone? (Choose one.)

   a) Today
   b) Yesterday
   c) _____ days ago (fill in the blank with a number)
   d) I can't remember.

3. If you complimented someone, what did you say?

Section 2

Why collectivists and individualists interact differently

1 As we learned in Section 1, collectivists and individualists have a variety of different norms and values. Therefore, it is not a surprise that they have different ways of interacting. In Section 2, we'll look at how people greet each other, the importance of context when talking to others, how people save face, and how they resolve conflicts. As we will see in this section, each of these topics has been a cause of misunderstanding between collectivists and individualists, and in at least one case, one of these topics contributed to the start of a war.

Unit 6

6.1 Forming in-groups:

needing or not needing party skills

Reading

2 People in individualist cultures (e.g., Canada, the United States, and Western Europe) have many in-groups. Because people in these places tend to be mobile, they often leave an in-group and join a new one (or several new ones). Unlike for collectivists, their in-groups are not necessarily determined by where they were born, the family that they were born into, or the place where they work or go to school. Individualists choose the in-groups that they want to join. For this reason, they don't feel great pressure to conform to any group. If a group wants a member to do something that they don't want to do, that person can easily quit that group and join another one. In sum, the individualists feel less attachment to any in-group; however, having less attachment to former groups means that individualists need to feel comfortable when meeting outsiders. Developing the social skills that are necessary for forming relationships with new people increases the possibility that they will be able to join new groups (Triandis et al, 1988). As long as they have the proper social skills and the motivation, they can join a number of different groups.

3 While collectivists feel happiest when their in-group does well, an individualist feels most pleasure when he himself is successful. An individualist might say, "What is best for me is very important."

4 A common perception is that Asians are shy and quiet among people that they do not know, and that Westerners (e.g., Europeans, Canadians and Americans) are outgoing and even noisy. In fact, researchers have found that both Asians and Westerners share this

perception. Researchers conducted a study of this topic at the Chinese University of Hong Kong. They discovered that both the Chinese students and American exchange students who were studying at this university felt that the American students were more outgoing and sociable, and the Chinese students were more passive, shy, and reserved. As a result of these characteristics, the Americans usually initiated conversations, and the Chinese responded (Smith and Bond, 1994).

French teens

Chinese teens

5 Why do Westerners appear more active in social situations, compared to Asians, who seem more passive? Some people mistakenly believe that the Asians are not friendly, do not want to talk to strangers, or just lack the motivation to start a conversation with a stranger. Cross-cultural psychologists reject these beliefs. As we have learned in Unit 3, an important in-group for Asians (collectivists) is their family and the friends of their family. Collectivists' in-groups do not change very often; i.e., they are unlikely to quit one in-group in order to join a new one. Also, they do not usually choose their in-groups. For this reason, there is little need for them to develop interpersonal skills for getting in groups. In other words, they don't need to develop skills (like starting a conversation with a stranger) that can be used to socialize with people who are outside of their in-groups. Westerners (individualists), on the other hand, frequently change in-groups. To do this, they need "party skills," which are techniques one might use to initiate and carry on a conversation while socializing with people whom one doesn't know well (Triandis, 1994b). In sum, people from individualist countries may seem more sociable, but it is just because they have to work hard in order to get into new groups. Well-developed social skills also help them maintain good relationships with members of their in-group, so that they can stay in that group as long as they would like to (Triandis et al, 1988). However, despite someone's efforts to stay in a certain group, there is always the risk that shifting loyalties among group members could force that person out of the group entirely. This is because individualist groups could be considered "fluid," so movement into and out of a group is always possible (and is expected, to some extent).

6.2 Complimenting:

A technique for joining a new group

6 Karen, an ESL teacher, has students from all over the world. During her class, the students are active and seem to enjoy her lessons. Many of them stay after class to talk to her and to get extra help. At the end of each term, she asks her students to write their

Karen's ESL class

opinions about her course. Her students from Europe often write compliments such as, "This was an interesting course," "I learned a lot," or "Great teacher!" However, many of her Asian students do not include much information and often just write "OK," or "no comment." This often confuses Karen because she works extremely hard to help her Asian students, and she wonders why they don't have any positive feedback about her course, or at least say that the course helped them in some way.

7 If Karen were aware of the research that has been done in the area of complimenting in collectivist and individualist cultures, her confusion and disappointment could be cleared up. Researchers have found that people from individualist cultures compliment each other quite frequently, while people from collectivist cultures make positive comments less often. Barnlund and Araki (1985) conducted interviews with university students in Japan and the United States. They were interested in learning how often the students were involved in a "complimenting" situation. They also analyzed what the topics of the compliments were, what expressions were used, who was involved, and whether the listener accepted the compliments.

8 They found that the Japanese gave or received a compliment, on average, only once every 13 days, whereas the Americans were involved with a compliment, on average, once every 1.6 days.

9 When the Japanese praised someone, it was about a wide variety of topics, e.g., actions, work and study, appearance, or skills. In contrast, the Americans' compliments were mainly about two topics: appearance or personality.

[10] The Japanese used rather limited and moderate descriptions, such as nice, good and all right. The Americans, however, used a wider range of adjectives, and the adjectives tended to be quite dramatic, such as beautiful, great, brilliant, super, and fantastic.

[11] Americans who received a compliment tended to accept the praise and/or extend it. Here is an example of both accepting and extending a compliment: If someone said to an American, "You wrote a really great essay," the American might accept it by saying, "Thank you," and extend it by saying, "I was happy with how it turned out too. I spent all weekend working on it."

[12] On the other hand, the researchers found that after receiving a compliment, the Japanese were likely to deny it, question its accuracy, say nothing, or just smile. In this example, when a Japanese was given the compliment "You wrote a really great essay," the Japanese would be apt to say, "No, it was a terrible essay," or "Do you really think so? I didn't think it was very good."

[13] Another finding from the study was that the closer the relationship between two people, the less likely the Japanese were to offer praise. However, in close relationships, the Americans were more likely to offer a compliment. Japanese complimented close friends only 16% of the time and acquaintances only 34%. Americans, on the other hand, complimented close friends 49% of the time and acquaintances 15%. When asked why they complimented to the extent which they did, the Japanese said that they felt it was unnecessary or unimportant to praise close friends. The Americans said that if they did not receive compliments in close relationships, they would feel insecure and uncomfortable, so they imagined that others would feel better if they received compliments too.

[14] There are two theories about these results. As discussed earlier, individualists often change groups. In order to join a new group, they might use compliments to charm outsiders and open new avenues of communication. For example, imagine that Jane is at a party and meets three interesting people, Sara, Jack and Bill, who are very close friends and who often travel together on vacations. Jane would like an invitation to join them on their next trip. Thus, during a conversation with them at the party, she could use compliments such as, "Jack, I really like the dessert that you brought to the party," or "Sara, I heard that the company which you work for is the best in its field," or "That's a very interesting idea, Bill." These compliments will help the others feel more comfortable around Jane, and she hopes, as a result, that they may ask her to join them. Collectivists, on the other hand, do not join new groups very often, so they do not feel a need to make an effort to develop this technique. That is one theory.

[15] The second theory concerning why collectivists spend less time giving compliments is related to group harmony and unity. As was mentioned earlier, group harmony is very important for collectivists, and as such, they try hard to not have conflicts

among their members. However, compliments can cause problems in a group because they might encourage comparisons. If Tom is with two friends, Ken and Ann, and Ann says, "Ken, I really think you are smart," Tom may feel that Ann doesn't believe that he is also smart. Perhaps, collectivists feel that, for the group to maintain harmony, the members should not make judgments about each other. When making even a positive judgment, there is a risk that other members might consider a compliment to be a comparison.

Part 1: Study guide for Unit 6

1. According to ¶ 2, why do people from individualist cultures need proper social skills?
   a) To help them join new in-groups
   b) To help their in-groups maintain harmony
   c) To help them conform to their in-group
   d) Because they feel pressure from their in-group

2. According to ¶ 3, an individualist might say, "What is best for me is important." Compare that comment to what a collectivist might say.

3. According to ¶ 4, what is the perception among Asians and Westerners?
   a) Westerners feel that Asians are shy around people that they don't know, but Asians think that they are not shy.
   b) Westerners feel that Asians are not shy around people that they don't know, but Asians think that they are shy.
   c) Westerners feel that Asians are shy around people that they don't know, and Asians also think that Asians are shy.

4. In ¶ 5, sentence 3, it states, "Cross-cultural psychologists reject these beliefs." What are the beliefs that they reject?

5. In ¶ 5, it mentions "party skills." Which of these are examples of party skills? (Choose three that are correct.)
   a) Saying "hello" to someone that you don't know
   b) Listening to a concert with other people
   c) Asking a new acquaintance a question about her hometown
   d) Giving a compliment to someone
   e) Eating pizza with a knife and fork
   f) Being a good dancer

6. Which of these are compliments? (See ¶ 6.) (Choose three that are correct.)
   a) You did an excellent job on your project.
   b) Your shoes need some polish.
   c) I like the way you handle your dog.
   d) Your cooking has really improved.
   e) You are not paying attention.
   f) That's a terrific haircut. Where did you get it?

7. Refer to ¶ 9-10. Who probably said this? Write ***a Japanese*** or ***an American*** in the blanks.
   a) "I thought that you sang the song well." ____________
   b) "I think you are very funny." ________________
   c) "Your sweater looks great."_____________
   d) "You cooked a good dinner."_____________

8. Statements A-D below refer to ¶ 13. Write ***True*** or ***False*** next to each.
   ___ A. Japanese tend to give a lot of compliments to their best friends.
   ___ B. Americans tend to give a lot of compliments to their best friends.
   ___ C. Japanese tend to give more compliments to people who are not close to them than they do to their best friends.
   ___ D. Americans tend to give more compliments to people who are not close to them than they do to their best friends.

9. According to ¶ 13-14, why do individualists compliment someone? (Choose the best answer.)
   a) They want to maintain group harmony.
   b) It is important to judge and compare their friends.
   c) They really feel the other person deserves the praise.
   d) It can help to make new friends and join a new group.

10. In ¶ 15, why do collectivists not give many compliments to someone? (Choose the best answer.)
    a) They do not feel that it is necessary.
    b) They don't think that the other person deserves it.
    c) They feel embarrassed.
    d) They want to compare friends.

11. Write one clarification question about a word, sentence, or idea that you do not understand in this unit. (If you understand everything, pretend that you don't.)

Part 2: Academic Vocabulary for Unit 6

Exercise 1

Words from context: Look at the paragraphs listed in the middle column of the chart below to find the words that have the meanings in the column on the right.

	Word	¶ *	Find the word that means . . .
1.		4	started something; began a process
2.		5	moving; changing
3.		7	participated in an activity or event
4.		12	say that some information is not true
5.		13	not confident

* **The symbol "¶" means paragraph.** You can find the word in that paragraph.

Exercise 2

Vocabulary Fill-in Exercise: Choose the words in Exercise 1 above to fill in the blanks below.

1. Sue couldn't come to class today because she was __________ in a car accident.

2. I never know what Tom is thinking because his opinions are always __________.

3. I'm sure that my roommate used my cell phone because when I asked him if he had, he didn't __________ it.

4. Many young people feel __________ when they move away from home for the first time.

5. Recently, there was some crime in our neighborhood. It was my next-door neighbor who __________ our discussions about installing street cameras and night-time security guards.

Exercise 3

Applied Vocabulary

1. Complete this sentence: Recently, I feel insecure about ______________________ .
   a) my financial situation
   b) my grade in this course
   c) my future
   d) other: ______________________________

2. What are you involved in these days? (Choose all that apply.)
   a) a sport
   b) a relationship with a girlfriend or boyfriend
   c) a club or other organization
   d) a job
   e) other: ______________________________

3. In your family, who usually initiated vacation planning: your mother, father, a sibling, or you?

4. Think about your childhood. Think about a time when you did something bad or wrong. And when your parents or teacher asked you if you had done it, you denied it. Describe what you had done that was bad or wrong.

5. Which of these sentences using shifting/shift has correct facts? (Choose all that apply.)
   a) Over the past 10 years, people have been shifting from using regular telephones to cell phones.
   b) A few years ago, people did not believe that the climate of the world has been getting hotter, but recently people's opinions have been shifting.
   c) Small cars used to be popular, but there has been a shift, and people now want bigger cars because they use less gas.
   d) In this class, we have been studying English, but next week we will shift to studying a different language.

Part 3: Preparation for discussion for Unit 6

Think about your answers to these questions. You do not have to write your answers.

1. Do you feel pressure to conform to your in-group members?
2. Which of these two situations would make you happier?
   Situation 1: On a test, you get a 100%, but your in-group members fail the test.
   Situation 2: On a test, you and your in-group members all get 85%.
3. Who are the members of your most important in-group in your country? How did you become a member of this in-group?
4. Do you feel comfortable meeting and talking to people who are not part of your in-group?
5. In ¶ 5, it mentions "party skills". Do you think that you have good party skills? Explain your answer.
6. In ¶ 11, it talks about accepting and extending praise. Let's say someone says to you, "I like your shirt." What could you say to accept and extend this praise?
7. If someone from your country said to you, "I like your essay," what would you say to them?
8. Do you expect your friends to compliment you? Why or why not?
9. Let's say that you gave me a compliment. For example, you tell me that you like my car. How would you feel if I didn't say anything to you in response? In other words, I was just silent.
10. Do your family members compliment you, and do you compliment them? Why or why not?

❖ For "Small-group Discussion" questions in the form of Students A, B, and C, see ***Supplementary Activities***, or download it free from www.ProLinguaAssociates.com.

❖ For "Whole-class Discussion" techniques and a suggested procedure, see the ***Supplementary Activities***, or download it free from www.prolinguaassociates.com.

❖ For "Applied Outside-class Interactions/Observations," see the ***Supplementary Activities***, or download it free from www.prolinguaassociates.com.

Part 4: A technique for writing good answers on tests

Give examples from your experiences, or from your culture or country, to show that you really understand.

Most instructors hope that their courses and the course textbooks are meaningful to students. You can use this technique to show your instructor that you understand the course material and that it is relevant to you. In this technique, you give examples from your experience, or from your culture or country, to show how the reading passage is related to your life.

Exercise 1

1) Read the "Information from a source" below.
2) Read the Sample Test Question.
3) Use a word or phrase from the box to fill in the blanks in the Student's answer.

> ***Information from a source***
>
> [People in individualist cultures] are, in general, more affluent than in collectivist cultures, and, because of this, they feel more independent … If they need help, for example, if they need someone to take care of their children while they are working, they usually have enough money to pay for it (Triandis, 1990).

Sample Test Question

Why do individualists tend to be more independent than collectivists?

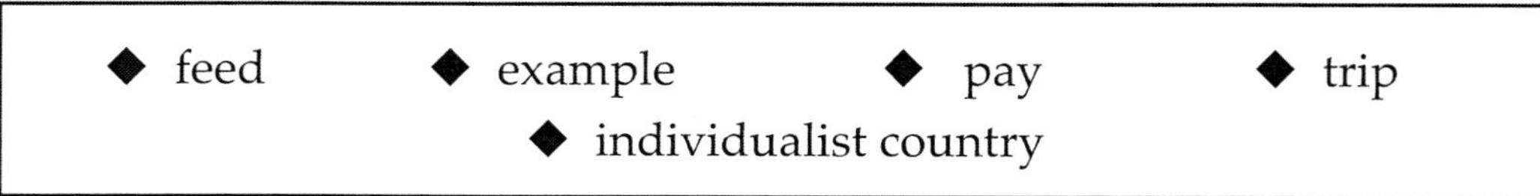

Student's answer

One reason why individualists tend to be more independent is because they have more money. As a result, they don't need the support from family members that collectivists do. They can pay other people to help them. For ________________, in my hometown, which is in an ____, when someone who has pets wants to take a__________________, they can ___________ a "pet-care company" to come to their house to ______________________ and play with it for an hour every day.

Exercise 2

Which of these students' answers have detailed examples from their country? Choose "Student A" or "Student B."

Sample Test Question: Explain how individualists get their in-groups.

Student A

Individualists get their in-groups by choosing them. For example, I am from an individualist country, and I always choose my friends.

Student B

Individualists get their in-groups by choosing them. For example, I am from an individualist country. Even though I love my family members and like my classmates, my best friends and in-group members are people whom I met a year ago while listening to two people playing music in a park. I started a conversation with some of the people in the audience and discovered that we shared similar interests. We soon became good friends.

Exercise 3

Which of these students' answers have detailed examples from their country? Choose "Student A" or "Student B."

Sample Test Question

Who is more likely to stay in their hometown: collectivists or individualists?

Student A

Collectivists tend to stay in their hometown. For example, in my country, Mexico, which is a collectivist country, my grandparents, parents, five uncles, seven aunts, and almost all my 19 cousins still live in my hometown. Only two of my cousins have moved to a different place.

Student B

Collectivists tend to stay in their hometown. For example, in my country, Mexico, which is a collectivist country, people rarely move away from their hometown.

Exercise 4

1) Read the source information in the three boxes below.

2) Choose 2 of the Sample Test Questions and write an answer that includes an example.

> ***Information from Source 1***
>
> A collectivist will behave differently toward someone, depending on whether that person is a member of their in-group or out-group (Kehe & Kehe, 2014).

Sample Test Question 1

How are individualists and collectivist different? (Include an example from your country in your answer.)

> ***Information from Source 2***
>
> Collectivists' in-groups do not change very often; i.e., they are unlikely to quit one in-group in order to join a new one. Also, they do not usually choose their in-groups. For this reason, there is little need for them to develop interpersonal skills for getting in groups. In other words, they don't need to develop skills (like starting a conversation with a stranger) that can be used to socialize with people who are outside of their in-groups. Westerners (individualists), on the other hand, frequently change in-groups. To do this, they need "party skills," which are techniques one might use to initiate and carry on a conversation while socializing with people whom one doesn't know well (Kehe & Kehe, 2014).

Sample Test Question 2

Who needs party skills more: collectivists or individualists? (Include an example from your country in your answer.)

> ***Information from Source 3***
>
> It is sometimes difficult for people to adjust to their home culture after returning from an extended stay in a different culture. This can be especially true for someone from a tight culture who is returning home after living in a loose culture, and vice versa (Kehe & Kehe, 2014).

Sample Test Question 3

What problems can people who have lived in foreign countries experience? (Include an example from your country in your answer.)

Part 5: Preview for Unit 7

Directions: Write your answers to these questions.

1. Imagine that you are talking to a good friend in your country about fashion. If you ask, "Do you think the colors of my new shirt look good on me?" and your friend answers, "Maybe they look good," what would you think?

   a) My friend likes my new shirt a lot.
   b) My friend is not sure if he likes my shirt.
   c) My friend does not like my shirt.

2. Is it important for you to save face? For example, let's say that you are in a meeting with 10 co-workers. You tell them about your idea for improving the company. If a co-worker says, "I don't think that that is a good idea," how would you feel?

   a) I would probably feel very embarrassed and upset.
   b) I would probably feel embarrassed and upset.
   c) I would probably feel a little embarrassed and upset.
   d) I wouldn't feel embarrassed and upset.

Unit 7

7.1 High- and Low-Context Cultures

Reading

1 Two American tourists were traveling in Japan during December. After spending a week in cold, damp Tokyo, they decided that they wanted to go someplace with warm, sunny weather. Studying their map of Japan, they noticed a southern island called Kyushu and asked their Japanese friend, Yumi, if that island would be warm in December.

2 Yumi took a deep breath and said, "Maybe it will be warm."

3 "Will it be warm enough to go swimming?" the Americans asked, full of hope.

4 Yumi hesitated and then responded, "Maybe it will be warm enough to swim."

5 Three days later, the tourists arrived in Kyushu. However, it wasn't warm at all; in fact, it was snowing! The Americans eventually learned that it is never warm enough to swim in Kyushu in December. They wondered why their Japanese friend had not been honest with them. (This was a personal experience by the authors of this book.)

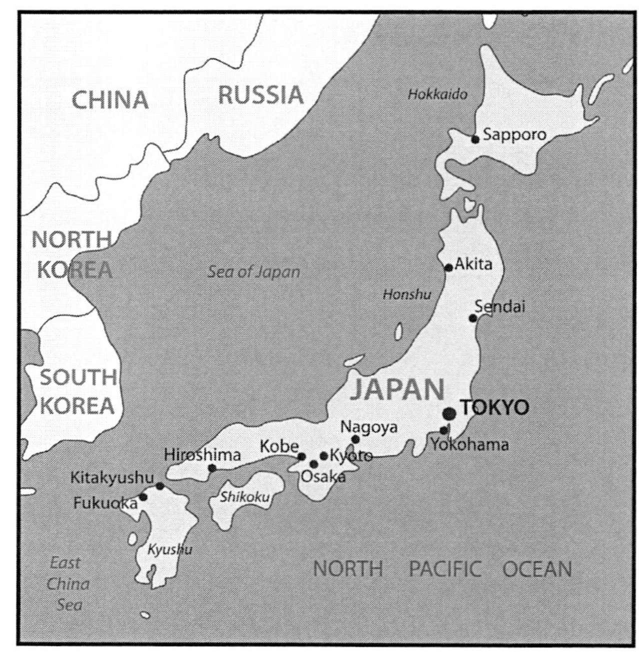

6 Anyone who knows the Japanese well would understand that Yumi was giving non-verbal signals to the Americans because, as a typical Japanese, she didn't want to directly tell them disappointing news. By breathing deeply and hesitating before answering, she expected them to not believe the exact words that she was saying but instead, to realize that, in a non-verbal way, she was actually giving them bad news about the chilly weather in Kyushu in December.

7 This is an example of **context**. "Context" includes such signals as the level of voice, silence, eye contact, smiling, breathing, gestures and body posture. People in collectivist cultures like to use context signals for communication because it is a way to help people avoid embarrassment and to maintain good relationships with others. The Japanese, for example, rarely say "no." In fact, according to one researcher, they have sixteen ways of expressing "no" without directly saying the word "no" (Triandis, 1994b).

8 Hall (1973) discusses the different manner in which two low-context and two high-context people will make a plan together. Here is a conversation between two people from a low-context country:

Dialog 1 *(low-context people)*

A: I know what we should do this evening. Let's go to a concert.

B: I think that I'd rather go a restaurant.

A: Hummm. Actually, this is the last night for the concert, and I'd really like to see it before it ends. We can go to a restaurant some other time.

B: That's true, but I really don't like that kind of music. I've got an idea. You could go to the concert alone, and we could meet at a restaurant later.

A: Good idea!

9 Here is a conversation between two people from a high-context country:

Dialog 2 *(high-context people)*

C: What do you think we should do tonight?

D: I'm not sure. I might need to finish writing a report. What do you think?

C: I heard that there is a concert in town.

D: I see. Do you think that it would be a good idea to go to it?

C: Maybe. What do you think?

D: Sure. It could be fun.

C: Will you have enough time to finish your report if we go?

D: I think I can finish it tomorrow morning.

C: I heard that the musicians are good, and tonight is the last night for it, so it's our last chance to hear it.

D: OK. Then let's go!

10 High-context speakers try to avoid expressing their preference directly because this could cause disharmony. In Dialog 2, Speaker C and D try to give each other opportunities to express a preference, and they don't try to impose their own ideas. If Speaker C were more direct about making a suggestion, it would cause D to be uncomfortable; this is because D would hesitate to reject C's idea. As a result, they try to make sure that they both agree with a plan, which is more important than satisfying one individual's preference.

11 In Dialog 1 above, between the low-context speakers, they try to make a plan that will satisfy the individual desires of both of them, even if it means doing separate activities for part of the evening. Thus, it's acceptable for a speaker to clearly express a preference.

12 It is easy to see that problems could arise if a low-context person (e.g., Speaker A in Dialog 1 above) and a high-context person (e.g., Speaker D in Dialog 2) tried to agree on a plan together. Speaker A would probably feel frustrated because Speaker D wouldn't clearly express a preference, and Speaker D would feel powerless because it would appear that Speaker A was acting bossy and trying to take control.

7.2 Non-verbal cues:

speaking directly or indirectly

13 Most collectivist cultures are considered **high context**. In these cultures, since people are, in general, homogeneous, they are familiar with each other's ways. As a result, they are able to easily "read" non-verbal messages. In other words, in many situations, they need fewer words to be spoken, as they can understand information from a variety of hints and signals.

Java tea and fried bananas

14 The following example, taken from Indonesian culture, helps clarify how high context works. A certain young Indonesian man and woman wanted to get married. Unfortunately, he was from a low social class, and she was from a high one. The general

pre-marriage custom was for the young man's mother to visit his girlfriend's mother. However, the girlfriend's mother did not approve of her daughter's lower-class fiancé, so during the visit, the girlfriend's mother served the young man's mother tea and bananas. Because people in this area of Indonesia never serve tea and bananas together, the young man's mother understood that the girlfriend's parents did not approve of the marriage. However, his own mother did not **lose face** (i.e., did not lose status or lose the respect of others) because the two mothers never directly discussed their opinions of their children's plans for marriage. As a result, the young man's mother did not feel openly rejected (Triandis, 1994a). From this example, we can see that it was the context, or situation, that made the combination of tea and bananas meaningful to the young man's mother. The girlfriend's mother was able to convey her thoughts without expressing her viewpoint verbally. This allowed the young man's mother to understand and still not lose face.

15 In contrast to the high-context nature of collectivist cultures, the individualist cultures tend to be **low context**. In Western Europe, Canada, the United States and Australia, where the societies are heterogeneous and where there is a greater variety of ways to interact, it is necessary for people to explain more directly what they mean. In other words, they must "spell things out." For individualists, the words that are said are of great importance. For collectivists, how a message is said is what is important; collectivists are apt to say what they imagine the other person wants to hear, but they might use non-verbal cues, such as hesitation, breathing deeply, or even serving tea and bananas, to express their true thoughts. Let's say an American mother did not want her son to marry his girlfriend, and she met with the girlfriend's mother. If she served some unusual combination of food and drinks (e.g., cake and an energy drink), the girlfriend's mother would never imagine that this combination had any specific meaning, other than that the son's mother combined food items in an odd way. Thus, the son's mother would have to spell things out by directly saying, "I don't think your daughter and my son are a good match."

16 Of course, every culture has variations of high and low context. For example, even though the United States is considered a low-context country, we can find examples of high-context use there. Take this situation, for example. If an American says to someone, "Let's have lunch sometime," it may not indicate a strong desire to have lunch with that person. Rather, the listener will probably realize that it is time to politely end the conversation and say "good-bye." Also, if a student visits the office of an American professor, when the professor is ready to end the conversation with the student, a glance at the clock on the wall might replace the verbal suggestion that, "It's time for you to leave." Even in a low-context culture, almost everyone will accurately interpret the professor's non-verbal cue.

7.3 Saving face:

avoiding embarrassment

17 As we can see from the examples above, non-verbal cues are ways to help someone to **save face**. In this phrase, "face" is a person's self-image. And "saving face" means supporting someone's positive self-image. People, especially collectivists, tend to avoid direct confrontations and prefer indirect comments and responses in order to "save their own face" (or their own self-image), or to "save someone else's face." This is because it is important that no one lose face.

18 The following is an example of a situation in Vietnam where someone saves face. In that country, when a woman says that her husband is dead, it might mean that he actually died, or it might mean that he has left her (perhaps because he decided to move out). Saying that he is dead helps her save face. Thus, in Viet Nam, if a woman says that her husband has died, it is inappropriate to ask her how or when he died, because she could lose face if she feels forced to explain that, in fact, he left her (DeCapua et al, 2004).

19 For collectivists, telling a "white lie" (i.e., a lie that is not serious and does not hurt anyone) is an acceptable strategy for maintaining harmony. However, for individualists, lying is generally considered less acceptable (Smith and Bond, 1994). Following is an example of this differing approach toward telling the truth. An American teacher was working in an Asian country and had to submit an official form to the university officials where she was teaching in order to get permission to take a trip. Unfortunately, a clerk at the university lost the form. A few weeks passed, but the American teacher did not get a response from the officials about her request, so she returned to the administration office to ask about her form. She was told that a high official was looking at her request but had not yet made a decision. Nobody told her that her form had been lost. The reason for this was that the administration did not want to lose face. If they had told her that they had lost the form, it would have appeared that they were incompetent. In sum, the administration was more concerned about saving face than about honest communication with this teacher (DeCapua et al, 2004).

Part 1: Study guide for Unit 7

1. In ¶ 1-4, what are two non-verbal signals that Yumi gave to the Americans?

2. Why did Yumi say to the Americans, "Maybe it will be warm enough to swim"? (Choose all that apply.)
   a) She really thought that it might be warm enough to swim.
   b) She knew that it wouldn't be warm enough to swim, but she did not want to disappoint them.
   c) She thought that it would be funny if they took their swimming suits to Kyushu in December.
   d) She thought that they would understand that it would not be warm enough if she breathed deeply, hesitated and said "maybe."

3. Answer the question at the end of each of the situations below. Write ***yes*** two times and ***no*** two times.

Situation 1

Alan is watching a DVD on his TV. His roommate, Brad, interrupts him and asks Alan if he could help him fix his computer. Alan continues to look at the TV, breathes deeply, and answers, "Sure. I can help you." Does Alan really want to help Brad? ________

Situation 2

Brad asks Alan if he can help him fix his computer. Alan answers, "Sure. I can help you." Does Alan really want to help Brad? ________

Situation 3

Anna tells Cindy that Jack asked her for a date, and she asks Cindy if she should go. Cindy says, "You might have a good time with him." Does Cindy really think that Anna should go on the date? ________

Situation 4

Anna tells Cindy that Jack asked her for a date, and she asks Cindy if she should go. Cindy looks surprised and smiles but doesn't say anything. So Anna asks her what she thinks. Cindy laughs and says, "You might have a good time with him." Does Cindy really think that Anna should go on the date? ________

4. Look at the four situations in Question 3 above again. In which of these situations is the context important to understand the person's opinion?
(Choose all that apply.) ______

5. After reading ¶ 7-9, choose the words from the box to fill in the chart about low- and high-context people.

◆ I want to …	◆ I'm not sure.	◆ It could be fun.
◆ We should …	◆ Maybe we could …	◆ What do you think?
◆ I really don't like …	◆ I know …	

Low-context people tend to say these.	**High-context people tend to say these.**

6. After reading ¶ 10-12, write ***high*** or ***low*** in each blank.

a) Maintaining harmony is important for ______-context speakers.

b) ______-context speakers tend to not say their opinions directly.

c) For ______-context speakers, it's important to directly express what they are thinking.

d) If their friend does not seem to want to do something, ______-context speakers will probably not want to do it either.

e) If two ______-context speakers cannot agree on a plan, they might do separate activities.

f) (This is about your personal opinion.) I feel more comfortable with ______-context speakers than ______-context speakers.

7. Write ***homogeneous*** (from ¶ 13) or ***heterogeneous*** (from ¶ 15) after each description.
   a) All the workers in the company come from Mexico.

      ____

   b) The students in the class are beginning level. ______________________________
   c) Some of my friends eat dinner at 6 p.m., but others eat at 10 p.m. __________
   d) Everyone in the Cowboy Club owns a horse.
   e) The dogs are of varied breeds, from huge guard dogs to tiny poodles. ______

8. Refer to ¶ 14. In which of these situations would the Indonesian man's mother lose face? (Choose all that apply.)
   a) The girlfriend's mother says, "I don't want your son to marry my daughter."
   b) The girlfriend's mother says, "I like your son, but you are from a different class, so our children should not get married.
   c) The girlfriend's mother says, "I am happy that your son will marry my daughter."

9. Imagine that Person A and B are from low-context cultures. Person B invited A to a party, but A doesn't want to attend. If A is silent for a few moments and then says, "I'll try to come," what will B probably think?
   a) B will think that A plans to attend if it is possible.
   b) B will understand that A does not want to attend.

10. Imagine that Person C and D are from high-context cultures. Person C invited D to a party, but D does not want to attend. If D is silent for a few moments and then says, "I'll try to come," what will C probably think?
    a) C will think that D plans to attend if it is possible.
    b) C will understand that D does not want to attend.

11. Which of these is a non-verbal signal? (Choose all that apply.)
    a) I nod my head up and down.
    b) I ask you to close the door.
    c) I point to the open window where the rain is coming in.
    d) While I am singing, you put your fingers in your ears.
    e) You ask me to stop singing.

12. In ¶ 15, the phrase "spell things out" appears. Which of these is an example of "spelling things out"?

    Situation

    Tom asks Mary for a date, but Mary does not like Tom because he is rude to almost everyone.

    a) She tells him, "I am not feeling well, so I can't go out."

    b) She tells him, "I would really like to, but I have a lot of homework to do."

    c) She tells him, "I don't want to go out with you because you have bad manners."

13. Which of these is an example of telling someone what that person wants to hear by using non-verbal cues to tell the truth, which is bad news? (Choose all that apply.)

    Situation

    Ken asks his professor if she thinks Ken will pass the course. The professor knows that Ken will fail.

    a) The professor is silent for a few seconds, then breathes deeply, and says, "You might pass this course."

    b) The professor says, "You might pass this course."

    c) The professor says, "I'm sorry, but your average is too low, so you can't pass."

14. In your own culture, if you want to politely end a conversation with someone, what do you do or say?

15. According to ¶ 17, a person can ___.

    a) only save his or her own face

    b) can only save someone else's face

    c) can save his or her own face and someone else's face

16. In ¶ 18, there is an example of saving face. Who saved face?

    a) The Vietnamese woman saved face because she would be embarrassed if people knew that her husband had left her.

    b) The people whom the Vietnamese woman is talking to saved face because they would feel embarrassed if they found out that her husband had decided to leave her.

    c) The Vietnamese woman's husband saved face because people would have a negative impression of him.

17. In ¶ 19, it mentions "white lie." Which of these is a white lie? (Choose all that apply.)

    a) Your roommate, who is a terrible cook, has made spaghetti for dinner. He asks you if you would like some. Although you are very hungry, you say, "No thanks. I just finished eating dinner."

    b) You borrowed your roommate's car. While you were trying to park it, you accidentally hit a pole, and it makes a dent in the car. The next day, your roommate notices the dent and asks you if you did it. You say that you did not do it.

    c) Your roommate borrows your car. When she returns it, she tells you that she thinks that she made a dent it in. You tell her that you think that actually you yourself had made the dent the week before even though you had not.

    d) You are at your friend's apartment. The phone rings, but she cannot answer it because she is busy, so you pick up the phone. It is her boyfriend, whom you do not like. You tell the boyfriend that your friend does not want to date him anymore.

18. In ¶ 19, it tells the story about the lost form at the university. Do you think that the clerk was telling a white lie?

19. Write one clarification question about a word, sentence, or idea that you do not understand in this unit. (If you understand everything, pretend that you don't.)

Part 2: Academic Vocabulary for Unit 7

Exercise 1

Words from context: Look at the paragraphs listed in the middle column of the chart below to find the words that have the meanings in the column on the right.

	Word	¶ *	Find the word that means . . .
1.	Impose	10	force people to accept something
2	Rejected	14	not chosen; not accepted
3	Interpret	16	understand the meaning of something that might be difficult for others to understand
4	Self-image	17	how you feel about yourself
5	inappropiate	18	not proper, or right, for the situation

* **The symbol "¶" means paragraph.** You can find the word in that paragraph.

Exercise 2

Vocabulary Fill-in Exercise: Choose the words in Exercise 1 above to fill in the blanks below.

1. Talking on a cellphone during class is considered __inappropiate__.
2. He is easy-going and open-minded unless he feels that people are trying to __impose__ their ideas on him. Then, he becomes stubborn.
3. Jim's girlfriend is mad at him, so he tries to call her. However, she won't answer her phone. Jim __interpret__ her behavior to mean that she is still angry.
4. After Lee's application was __rejected__ by his first job choice, he applied for a different one.
5. In high school, Karen was a good soccer player, she starred in the school play, and she got excellent grades. All these successes gave her a positive __self-image__.

Exercise 3

Applied Vocabulary

1. My brother is afraid to ask any girls out for a date. He also does not want to ask his boss to pay him more money. My brother probably ___.

   a) has a high self-image
   b) has a low self-image

2. In your country, is it inappropriate to wear shoes inside someone's home? ________

3. Which of these is an example of someone who was rejected? (Choose all that apply.)

   a) Tom wanted to join the military, but the doctor said that he had stomach problems, so the military would not take him.

   b) I got a telephone call, and the caller wanted me to give money to a charity. I told the caller that I did not have any money to donate.

   c) My friend has to work late tonight, so I decided to go to a movie alone.

   d) Mike had a problem with his car. I told him that I could give him a ride to school, but he said that he would take a bus.

   e) During her vacation, Ann could go surfing, shop or read a book. In the end, she decided to read.

4. Let's say that you are a parent. What rule do you think that you would impose on your teenage children?

5. Let's say that you are a boss. Late one day in your office, you tell a worker that he cannot go home yet because he needs to finish some work. As he is leaving your office, he slams your door. In other words, he closes it loudly. How would you interpret his behavior?

Part 3: Preparation for discussion for Unit 7

Think about your answers to these questions. You do not have to write your answers.

1. Can you understand why Yumi didn't tell the truth, or do you think that her actions were strange?
2. In ¶ 8-9, it gives examples of a low-context and high-context conversation. When you are making plans with a friend, are you more like the low- or high-context people? Give some examples.
3. Do you ever feel uncomfortable or frustrated when you make plans because the other person is a high- or low-context person? Give some examples.
4. Imagine that you wanted to marry someone, but your parents did not want you to. What do you think that your parents would do?
5. Explain an example of a situation in which you or someone you knew lost face.
6. Is your country considered to be homogeneous or heterogeneous? Do you like it that way? Or do you wish it were different?
7. Imagine that you are feeling cold because a window is open. Do you know ways to non-verbally show someone that you are cold?
8. Let's say that I invited you to a party at my place next weekend, but you do not want to come. What would you say to me?
9. In ¶19 it talks about white lies. Tell me a white lie now.
10. In ¶19, it tells about a problem that an American teacher had when trying to get a form from an office at her university. Do you think that this situation could happen in your country?

❖ For "Small-group Discussion" questions in the form of Students A, B, and C, see ***Supplementary Activities***, or download it free from www.ProLinguaAssociates.com.

❖ For "Whole-class Discussion" techniques and a suggested procedure, see the ***Supplementary Activities***, or download it free from www.prolinguaassociates.com.

❖ For "Applied Outside-class Interactions/Observations," see the ***Supplementary Activities***, or download it free from www.prolinguaassociates.com.

Part 4: A technique for writing good reports and answers on tests

Give your opinion and support it with source information (Part 1).

On academic assignments, for example, tests or reports, students are asked to give their opinion. However, instructors do not want to read just the students' opinions. Instead, they want to see how well students can support their opinions with information from a source. This is a type of "critical thinking" skill that is important in college courses.

In this exercise, you will give your opinion, and then you will support it by paraphrasing information from this book. When giving your opinion, instead of always writing, "I think …" or "I believe …" or "I feel …," you will introduce your opinion with other, more academic expressions.

In this box are useful expressions to use to introduce your opinion.

Expressions for giving your opinion

- In my opinion, . . .
- It seems to me that . . .
- It seems obvious that . . .
- It appears that . . .
- Clearly, . . .

Exercise 1

Read "Party Invitations."

Party Invitations

About six months ago, a group of international students arrived at a Canadian college campus. Soon after arriving, several of these students joined the International Friendship Club at the college, which included both international students and Canadian students. The purpose of this club was to develop a better understanding among people from different cultures. The members spent a lot of time together in a variety of activities, including doing sports, camping, having parties, and visiting nearby places of interest. One day, some members decided to organize a dinner party for the following Friday at the apartment of one of the members, Ken. Three days prior to the party, two members, Sue and Angela, were comparing their plans. Sue said that she had wanted to spend that weekend working on a report for her history class, but she didn't want to disappoint the other members, especially Ken, whom she considered to be a close friend, so she planned to attend. Angela, on the other hand, was planning to skip the party in order to go to a concert with her roommate and some other students who lived in her apartment building.

Exercise 2

Read this essay question about "Party Invitations": Do you think Sue and Angela were collectivists or individualists? Support your opinion by using information from *Cultural Differences*.

Exercise 3

Below is a student's answer to the essay question in Exercise 2. Use the words from the box below to fill in the blanks for the answer.

◆ According to	◆ clearly	◆ In this case
◆ it appears that Angela	◆ seems obvious that	

It ______________________________ Sue is a collectivist. Even though she preferred to stay home and study, she decided to join the party. ______________________ *Cultural Differences*, collectivists feel that they are part of a group and, therefore, are willing to respect the group's goals. _________________________, the group's goals were to have a dinner party, and Sue decided not to pursue her own goal (of studying) in order to support the group in achieving its goal (of having a get-together). On the other hand, _____ _____________________________________is an individualist. As Kehe and Kehe (2014) mention, individualists tend to agree with the statement, "My goal is to do whatever I think is worth doing." ________, Angela's goal is to go to a concert with a different group of people, and she plans to pursue that plan.

◆ Kehe and Kehe state that if	◆ There is evidence that
◆ certainly	◆ As explained in *Cultural*

________________________________ Sue is a collectivist, and Angela is an individualist. ______________________________ *Differences*, collectivists tend to belong to just one club and are loyal to that one club. Sue fits that description. She plans to attend the dinner party due to her sense of loyalty to the International Friendship Club and to her friend, Ken. However, Angela ________________________has the characteristics of an individualist. She has more than one in-group: the Friendship Club as well as her friends in her apartment building. ______________________________

______the goals of an individualist's in-group do not match those of the individualist, they will change in-groups. Since the club's goal of having a dinner party did not match Angela's goal for that weekend, she decided to join her other in-group.

Reference

Kehe, D., & Kehe, P. (2014). *Cutural Differences*. Brattleboro, Vt.: Pro Lingua.

Exercise 4

Read *Family Rules or Freedom* and write an answer to the essay question at the end of it.

Famiy Rules or Freedom

Judy was an American high school student, and when she was 15 years old, she had a homestay in Mexico with a middle-class family for one month. Judy became good friends with her 14-year-old host sister, Rosa, and with Rosa's friends. In general, Judy was enjoying her experience, but she felt frustrated because her host family had more rules than her real family had. Sometimes she suggested to Rosa and her friends that they do something unusual, but they felt uncomfortable and refused to discuss it if it broke a rule in Rosa's family. One day, Judy became excited because she heard that a famous American rock group was supposed to play in the city the next week. Judy suggested that she, Rosa and Rosa's friends go. They all said it sounded like fun, but Rosa and her friends were sure that their parents would never let them attend a concert late at night. Judy recommended that they tell their parents that they were planning to spend the night at another person's house and then secretly go to the concert. Rosa and her friends refused to even consider that. As a result, Judy felt disappointed in them (Brislin et al, 1986).

Essay question

How would you explain to someone the reasons why Judy and Rosa have the conflict about going to the concert? Support your opinion by using information from *Cultural Differences*. In your answer, you could include information about norms, collectivism, and individualism, tight and loose cultures and conformity.

◆ Use Expressions for giving your opinion (in the box). Underline the expressions in your answer.

Expressions for giving your opinion

- In my opinion, . . .
- It seems to me that . . .
- It seems obvious that . . .
- It appears that . . .
- Clearly, . . .

Part 5: Preview for Unit 8

Directions: Write your answers to these questions.

1. Imagine that, in your college class, your instructor tells the students that he needs two students to help him on the weekend. Your friend raises her hand to volunteer and says that she is sure that you would also volunteer to help. However, you don't want to volunteer. What would you do?

   a) Tell the instructor and your friend that you can't help him.

   b) Just smile and say nothing and hope that the instructor understands that you can't help him.

2. Imagine that you are in a writing class. One day, your instructor tells you to read the essay of your classmate Tony and to give him some comments about it. Tony will be able to use your comments to improve his essay and perhaps get a better grade. Tony's essay is not interesting, and it has a lot of grammar mistakes. What will you say to Tony?

   a) Tony, I think that, in general, your essay is good and interesting.

   b) Tony, I think that you need to make it more interesting. Also, you have some grammar mistakes, here, and here and here …

3. Imagine that you are in a writing class. One day, your instructor tells Tony to read your essay and to give you some comments. You will be able to use his comments to improve your essay and perhaps get a better grade. You don't think that your essay is very good, and you think that it probably has some grammar mistakes.

- ◆ How would you feel if Tony says, "I think that, in general, your essay is good and interesting"?

- ◆ How would you feel if Tony says, "I think that you need to make it more interesting. Also, you have some grammar mistakes, here and here … " ?

Unit 8

8.1 Sending messages

How it is said rather than what is said

Reading

1 A misunderstanding between a high-context individual and low-context one can cause serious problems and, on rare occasions, even death. In January 1991, after Iraq invaded Kuwait, an American government official, James Baker, met with Tariq Aziz, an advisor to Iraq's president, Saddam Hussein. Baker, who is from a low-context culture, said calmly and directly, "If you do not move out of Kuwait, we will attack you." However, Aziz, who is from a high-context culture, paid more attention to *how* Baker spoke, and he paid little attention to the exact words in Baker's warning. Later, Aziz reported to his boss, Saddam Hussein, that Baker did not look angry. "The Americans are just talking. They will not attack us." Aziz had thought that if Baker were serious about attacking, he would have yelled, pounded his fists on the table, and perhaps thrown some objects across the room in anger. However, Baker felt that a good diplomat should remain cool and should just state his position clearly. Saddam decided to keep his soldiers in Kuwait, based on his advisor's interpretation that Baker's warning was just a fake. Six days later, Saddam was surprised when the Americans attacked, killing thousands of Iraqis and causing $130 billion in damages to Kuwait and $200 billion in damages to Iraq (Triandis, 1994a).

2 Classmates and roommates from two different cultures can also have misunderstandings that are similar to that of Aziz and Baker (described above), although the result may not be as catastrophic as was the case in that previous example about Kuwait and Iraq. Take this example which involves a communication breakdown between an Asian and an American student. Mariko, an Asian student from a collectivist culture, was a new student at an American university. She became good friends with Linda, one of her American classmates. During one of the classes, the professor asked everyone if two

students would volunteer to do some research for him in his office the next morning. Linda raised her hand to volunteer and told the professor that perhaps Mariko, who was sitting next to her, might also be willing to help. Mariko hesitated to answer, smiled, and said that she did not think that her English was good enough and that, perhaps, someone else would be better. Linda said that she was sure Mariko was capable and told the professor that they would both do the research. The next morning, Mariko did not come to the professor's office, so Linda had to do all of the research alone. Later, she saw Mariko and asked her why she had not shown up. Mariko apologized and said that she had had a lot of other work and did not feel capable of doing that kind of research. Linda became frustrated and asked Mariko why she had not clearly explained her situation in the class. Mariko just looked down and didn't say anything (Cushner and Brislin, 1996).

Mariko *Linda*

3 The situation described above is another case in which someone from a high-context culture felt hesitant to express what was on her mind. Mariko felt that it would be wrong to refuse the professor and that it might embarrass him if she did. She tried to convey her reluctance by hesitating, smiling and expressing doubt in an indirect manner. However, Linda did not perceive this. She had expected Mariko to answer as an American would, by saying, "No, I'm too busy" if she really did not want to work on the research project. As a result, Linda felt that Mariko had been dishonest or deceptive. Mariko, however, was just trying to not embarrass anyone.

8.2 Giving opinions

honesty vs. harmony

4 A teaching technique that is commonly used in writing classes in the U.S. is writing groups, in which classmates evaluate each other's work; this is often referred to as "peer editing." Needless to say, ESL students who enroll in English Composition courses are expected to participate in this type of activity too. On the surface, it would appear that ESL students from collectivist cultures would easily function in writing groups since they are accustomed to group work in their own cultures. However, according to a study, for some students from Asian countries, peer-editing activities may cause some trouble.

5 Educators have found that students can benefit from engaging in group discussions about their own writing, from learning different thinking strategies from other members, and from the combined expertise that the group can offer. Educators in the collectivist Asian countries and in the individualist U.S. and Canada tend to agree on the value of group work and on the benefits that can be gained from it. However, the similarities stop there because the concept of "a group" in a collectivist culture is different from "a group" in an individualist one. Therefore, a group composed of a mixture of Asians and Americans can result in major frustration on both sides (Carson and Nelson, 1994).

6 In an American college composition class, two Asian students and two American students were assigned to a group. The four students were told to peer-edit each member's essay by following these steps:

1) One member should give a copy of his essay to the other three members.
2) After reading the essay, each member should make comments about the quality of the paper, including its strong and weak points.
3) After discussing the first member's essay, the group should repeat Steps 1 and 2 with the other three members' work.

7 Observing the group, we can find some differences in how the two Asians and two Americans interacted with each other.

8 After reading one of their peer's essays, the Asian students tended to say what they thought the writer wanted to hear, or they did not say anything at all. They seldom offered advice on how the writer could make improvements. It seemed that they were afraid of hurting the writer's feelings if they were too critical, so if they made comments at all, they were generally positive ones. On the other hand, the Americans were direct in their remarks. They pointed out specific weaknesses in the other essays and made suggestions for improvement.

9 After completing the assignment, the members were interviewed separately to find out their reactions to the experience. The Asians said they felt that the Americans were rude because they were too critical and did not seem to consider the writer's feelings. Thus, by the end of the activity, the Asians had a negative attitude about this type of group work. In contrast, the Americans said the Asians were not deep thinkers because they could not offer criticisms of the essays; the Americans' impressions of the Asians was that either they did not talk at all or they made general, positive comments that were not helpful. The Americans concluded that the Asians were probably not honest in this type of group activity. (This was a personal experience by the authors of this book.)

Part 1: Study guide for Unit 8

1. In ¶ 1, there is a story about James Baker and Tariq Aziz. Who do you think made a mistake and caused the Gulf War? Explain your opinion.

2. In ¶ 2, it says in the second to last sentence "Linda became frustrated …." Why was Linda frustrated?
   a) She had to do all the work herself.
   b) She did not understand why Mariko did not give her honest opinion.
   c) Her professor was angry.
   d) She thought that Mariko's English was hard to understand.

3. In ¶ 4, it mentions "peer editing." What is it?
   a) Students show their essays to their instructor and talk about them.
   b) Students show their essays to a classmate and talk about them.
   c) Students write an essay with a classmate.

4. According to ¶ 5, who thinks that group work is useful?
   a) individualist educators
   b) collectivist educators
   c) both individualist and collectivist educators.

5. Below is a summary of the peer-editing experience in ¶ 6-9. Fill in the blank with "OK" if the statement is correct. If it is not correct, write the correction above the mistake.

two Asians and two Americans

___ ***Statement 1)*** The students participated in groups of ~~all Asians or all Americans~~.

OK ***Statement 2)*** First, the members read one of the student's essays.

___ ***Statement 3)*** After reading that essay, the members explained only what was good about it.

___ ***Statement 4)*** The Asian students usually did not point out mistakes in the students' essays.

___ ***Statement 5)*** Sometimes the American students did not say anything.

___ *Statement 6)* The Asian students liked the type of comments that the Americans made.

___ *Statement 7)* The Asian students' comments usually were not helpful for the writers to improve their essays.

___ *Statement 8)* The American students thought the Asian students' comments were not deep.

___ *Statement 9)* The American students thought that maintaining group harmony was more important than telling the truth.

6. Write one clarification question about a word, sentence, or idea that you do not understand in this unit. (If you understand everything, pretend that you don't.)

Part 2: Academic Vocabulary for Unit 8

Exercise 1

Words from context: Look at the paragraphs listed in the middle column of the chart below to find the words that have the meanings in the column on the right.

	Word	¶ *	Find the word that means . . .
1.		3	preference to not do something
2.		5	high-level skill or knowledge about a subject
3.		5	important; serious
4.		2	able to do something well
5.		8	detailed; exact

* **The symbol "¶" means paragraph.** You can find the word in that paragraph.

Exercise 2

Vocabulary Fill-in Exercise: Choose the words in Exercise 1 above to fill in the blanks below.

1. Before buying a used car, it is a good idea to find someone who has ____________ in auto mechanics to help you make a smart choice.

2. Even though I don't have a ____________ plan for my next vacation, I know that I want to go to a warm place.

3. The child showed ____________________ to ride her bicycle the first time, so her parents helped her.

4. After having a __________________ argument with his friend, Jay could not sleep that night.

5. After passing her driving test, Jan felt _______________ of driving across the country.

Exercise 3

Applied Vocabulary

1. When you were younger, what did you have a reluctance to do? ______________
____

2. What is the name of a person who had a major influence on you?
_________________________________ How did that person affect you?

3. Which of these activities do you feel capable of doing?
   a) swimming 50 meters
   b) passing this class
   c) flying an airplane
   d) cooking noodles
   e) fixing a computer

4. Which of the following describes a specific problem? (Choose all that apply.)
   a) Athletes suffer too many injuries in sports.
   b) My computer will not go on sleep mode.
   c) Mr. Kim's dog barks whenever the mailman comes to his house.
   d) My neighbor is not a good person.
   e) There are more and more cases of bad weather nowadays.
   f) This pizza doesn't have enough cheese.
   g) Wars cause a lot of damage around the world.

5. Name a person whom you know that has an expertise in something? __________
What does that person have an expertise in?

Part 3: Preparation for discussion for Unit 8

Think about your answers to these questions. You do not have to write your answers.

1. Explain an example of a situation in which you sent non-verbal signals to someone.
2. Is group work popular in schools in your country? Explain.
3. Do you do peer-editing in your country?
4. Do you enjoy doing group work, or do you prefer teacher lectures? Explain.
5. If you did peer editing with some Americans, would you do it more like the Asians or Americans? Explain.
6. Do you think that politicians in your country negotiate more similarly to the Iraqi diplomat or to the American diplomat in ¶ 1?
7. In the situation about Mariko and Linda in ¶ 2, if you were a classmate of Linda's, and she volunteered for you to do some extra work, but you didn't want to do it, what would you do?

❖ For "Small-group Discussion" questions in the form of Students A, B, and C, see ***Supplementary Activities***, or download it free from www.ProLinguaAssociates.com.

❖ For "Whole-class Discussion" techniques and a suggested procedure, see the ***Supplementary Activities***, or download it free from www.prolinguaassociates.com.

❖ For "Applied Outside-class Interactions/Observations," see the ***Supplementary Activities***, or download it free from www.prolinguaassociates.com.

Part 4: A technique for writing good reports and answers on tests

Give your opinion and support it with source information (Part 2).

In Unit 7, you wrote an essay explaining why Judy, an American high school student, was upset at her Mexican host-sister, Rosa. For this exercise, you will read about a problem between an American businessman and his Korean secretary. After you read the story, you will explain why they are having a problem, and you will use academic expressions to introduce your opinions.

Exercise

Read "A Manager and Secretary Conflict" and write an answer to the essay question below it.

A Manager and Secretary Conflict

An American named Todd is a manager of an American company in Korea. His secretary is a Korean woman, Chungmin, and they seemed to have a friendly relationship. One day, he asked Chungmin to type a letter for him, but unfortunately, she forgot to do it. Although Todd didn't think that it was a serious mistake, he felt that he needed to let her know that she hadn't done it. At lunch time, he saw her in the lunchroom sitting with some of the other employees; he approached her and explained that she hadn't typed the letter that he had asked for. After this incident, Chungmin began to act cooler toward Todd and even a bit defiant. If she had to bring some files to his office, she tended to avoid making eye contact with him, and when she left, she closed his door quite loudly. She also seemed to be irritable when he was around her. For the first time in many years, she even missed some work-days by saying that she was sick.

After Chungmin returned to work from her days off due to sickness, Todd asked her to come into his office to talk about why she has been acting so unusual recently. Chungmin, with a look of misery on her face, told him that the lunchroom incident had had an effect on her. Todd replied that the mistake with the letter was not a serious one and told her not to worry about it. However, Chungmin continued to act cold around Todd, and in fact, missed several more days of work due to sickness over the next few weeks (Cushner & Brislin, 1996).

Essay question

Why do you think Chungmin and Todd were having a problem? Support your opinion by using information from *Cultural Differences.*

- Explain at least two reasons.
- Use Expressions for giving your opinion (in the box). Underline the expressions in your answer.

Expressions for giving your opinion

- In my opinion, . . .
- It seems to me that . . .
- It seems obvious that . . .
- It appears that . . .
- Clearly, . . .

Part 5: Preview for Unit 9

Directions

Read the "Situation" in the box below and answer the question under it.

Situation

You are the president of a company. One day, one of your workers, Ms. A, tells you that two other workers, Mr. B and Mr. C, had a big argument while they were working. In the argument, Mr. B said that Mr. C was not working hard enough.

What would you do about this situation? (Choose one.)

a) I (as the president of the company) would have a meeting with the two workers, Mr. B and Mr. C, together to talk about the situation and to find out if it is true that Mr. C was not working hard enough.

b) I (as the president of the company) would have a meeting alone with Mr. B and tell him that it's important for him to try to get along with Mr. C and to try to help him. Then, I would have a meeting alone with Mr. C and tell him that it's important for him to try to get along with Mr. B and to try to help him.

Unit 9

9.1 Resolving Conflicts

Meet separately or face-to-face.

Reading

1 A difference in values (in this case, harmony for collectivists and independence for individualists) was demonstrated in a study of 56 Chinese university students in Hong Kong and 60 American students in New York. Researchers gave the students this scenario (i.e., imaginary situation):

Hong Kong University

Scenario

2 A president of a company had a meeting with some members of his advertising department. During the meeting, one of the workers insulted a co-worker by saying, "I think that your work is terrible. You are doing an awful job."

Question: How would you resolve this conflict between the two workers?

3 The American university students said that the president should have a meeting with the two workers together and find out the truth. They felt that the president could solve the conflict most efficiently by analyzing whether the worker actually was doing terrible work.

4 The Chinese students, on the other hand, said that the president should meet the two workers separately. By doing this, there would be less risk that the conflict would get worse. Meeting separately would also decrease the possibility of having future problems between the two. The Chinese students felt that learning the truth about whether one worker was terrible or not was less important than maintaining harmony and unity among the workers (Bond, Wan, Leung, and Giacalone, 1985).

9.2 Handling personal problems

Confrontation, submission or compromise

5 Imagine that you have personal problems with a teacher, with your best friend, and with your father. How would you handle these problems? Read the three scenarios below. Then choose your responses.

6 ***Scenario 1***

Imagine that you are in your classroom sitting next to your best friend. During the lesson, the two of you are chatting about something exciting that recently happened to you. The teacher has to stop often to tell both of you to stop talking, but because you think the lesson is rather dull, the two of you continue conversing and joking with each other. For a few days, in class, you and your friend continue to have these conversations during the lessons. Finally, one day the teacher stops her lesson, tells you that you have interrupted too often and that you will be punished. She says that you will not be allowed to go on the school trip with the other students. You do not want to miss the trip, and you feel that the teacher is unfair because other students were also having private conversations, but the teacher didn't punish them. How do you respond to your teacher? (Put an ✓ in the blank next to your choice.)

___ *(Confrontation)*
I tell the teacher that she is not fair and that I should be allowed to go on the school trip.

___ *(Submission)*
I stop talking to my friend and decide not to chat anymore during the lessons with the hope that the teacher will change her mind and let me go on the trip.

___ *(Compromise)*
I tell the teacher that I realize that I was talking too much. Then, I ask the teacher if I can go on the trip if I do not chat during the lessons in the future.

7 *Scenario 2*

You are worried about an English test that you will take at your school in a week. If you fail the test, you won't be promoted and will need to repeat the level for the next year, but you very much want to move to the next level with all your classmates. Even though you do not like English, you have decided to study hard for this test. Fortunately, the top student in the class is your best friend, and she has promised to help you study for the test later that day. You are confident that, with your friend's help, you will be able to pass the test. After school, by chance, you run into your friend and remind her about her promise to help you. However, she casually says that she won't be able to do that after all because she is busy, and she had promised some other students to help them. She doesn't even apologize to you! You are completely surprised. How do you respond to your friend?

___ ***(Confrontation)***
I tell her that I am very angry. I tell her that she promised to help me, but now she is really disappointing me. I ask her why she is doing this.

___ ***(Submission)***
I don't show any disappointment. I tell her that I understand why she can't help me. Then I quickly walk away.

___ ***(Compromise)***
I ask her if she could spend just an hour to help me with the most difficult content on the test. And I say that I'll buy a movie ticket for her later.

8 *Scenario 3*

You find out from your friends at school that they get more spending money every week from their parents than you do. Because of your tight budget, you sometimes don't have enough money to go to movies and do other activities with friends, and this makes you frustrated. That evening, you ask your father to increase the amount for your spending money. However, he responds by complaining about you. He says that you don't spend enough time at home with your family and that you don't help with work around the house. He also says that you should spend more time studying for exams and less time having fun with your friends, so he refuses to increase your spending money. This is upsetting to you because you feel it's very important for you to get together with your friends, but you need more money in order to do it in an appropriate way. How do you respond to your father?

___ *(Confrontation)*

I tell my father that I do not accept his viewpoint at all and ask him to talk to other parents in order to find out how much spending money their kids get.

___ *(Submission)*

I decide to spend more time at home in the future in order to make my father happy, and I don't talk about increasing my spending money anymore.

___ *(Compromise)*

I promise to do more work at home if he will agree to increase the amount of spending money that I receive.

Exercise 1

From your answers above, fill in the blanks with your choices, a, b, or c.

___ 1. How would you respond to your teacher in Scenario 1?
a) confrontation b) submission c) compromise

___ 2. How would you respond to your best friend in Scenario 2?
a) confrontation b) submission c) compromise

___ 3. How would you respond to your father in Scenario 3?
a) confrontation b) submission c) compromise

9 In fact, researchers used the scenarios described above to analyze how young people in collectivist and individualist countries would resolve personal problems that involved another person. The subjects for this study were 261 teenagers from two different countries: Indonesia, a collectivist country, and Germany, an individualist one. The researchers described those three different scenarios, and the subjects were told to choose one of the following three methods for responding to the dilemmas:

Confrontation

The subject would disagree with the other person and would explain that they are not fair and should change their mind.

Submission

The subject would agree with the other person and not try to change that person's mind.

Compromise

The subject would agree with the other person but would suggest that they "make a deal," in which each of them makes a change in some way.

10 The results below indicate how differently people in a collectivist and individualist culture respond to the three scenarios described above. (The results are rounded off to whole numbers.)

Results

◆ **Scenario 1**: a conflict with a teacher

	Confrontation	Submission	Compromise
Indonesians	7%	22%	71%
Germans	30%	13%	57%

◆ ***Scenario*** **2**: a conflict with your best friend

	Confrontation	Submission	Compromise
Indonesians	35%	31%	34%
Germans	62%	16%	17%

◆ ***Scenario*** **3**: a conflict with your father

	Confrontation	Submission	Compromise
Indonesians	4%	63%	33%
Germans	28%	9%	64%

11 Few Indonesians chose confrontation with a teacher (7%) or father (4%), but many chose confrontation with a friend (35%). More than 60% of them chose submission in the conflict with the father. These results would be consistent with the collectivists' norms of showing obedience and respect to superiors, and with treating peers as equals.

12 Interestingly, the Germans were less likely to choose submission in the conflict with the father (9%) than with either the teacher (13%) or friend (16%). As we can see from this, the Germans were actually more likely to choose submission to a friend (16%) than to the father (9%). The researchers suggested that the reason for this result was the desire of German youths to gain independence from their family, a characteristic of individualists. As they weaken their family bonds, the relationship with peers tends to become stronger; they begin to see their peers as a valuable source of social support (Haar and Krahe, B, 1999).

Part 1: Study guide for Unit 9

(Questions 1 and 2 are about ¶ 1-4.)

1. Why did the Americans feel that the boss should meet the workers together? (Choose all that apply.)
   a) He wanted to hear one worker's side of the story, then the other's side. He could then ask questions and then perhaps decide who was lying.
   b) He wanted the worker who was right to see the other worker get punished.
   c) He wanted to explain to both of them together that they should not have disagreements.

2. Why did the Chinese students feel that the boss should meet the workers separately? (Choose all that apply.)
   a) If they were angry at each other, they might start arguing again if they were in the same room.
   b) He wanted to know why both of the workers were doing terrible work.
   c) He wanted to explain to each of them separately that it's important for them to get along.

3. Read the statements and fill in ***confrontation, submission,*** or ***compromise***.

____________________ a) I understand. You are right. I'll wash the dishes and do my homework.

____________________ b) I understand. If I wash all of the dishes after dinner and do all of my homework, then can I watch TV?

____________________ c) Why do I always have to wash dishes every day? Why doesn't my brother have to wash them sometimes?

____________________ d) I'm sorry. I won't do that anymore.

____________________ e) That's not fair. I really need to do that, so you cannot stop me.

____________________ f) OK. I have a suggestion. If I stop playing my music so loudly during these next two weeks, can I go to the concert next month?

For Questions 7-9, look at the results in the charts in ¶ 10.

4. Who is more likely to choose submission?
   a) Indonesians b. Germans

5. Who is more likely to choose confrontation?
   a) Indonesians b. Germans

6. In which scenario did the Germans compromise more than the Indonesians?

   ____

7. According to ¶ 12, we can conclude that the German students __________.
   a) consider their teachers to be a part of their in-group
   b) consider their fathers to be part of their in-group
   c) consider their friends to be a part of their in-group

8. Write one clarification question about a word, sentence, or idea that you do not understand in this unit. (If you understand everything, pretend that you don't.)

Part 2: Academic Vocabulary for Unit 9

Exercise 1

Words from context: Look at the paragraphs listed in the middle column of the chart below to find the words that have the meanings in the column on the right.

	Word	¶ *	Find the word that means . . .
1.		1	a situation that is imaginary but could be true
2.		3	thinking about or looking at something carefully in order to understand it better
3.		7	moved to a better or higher-level position
4.		9	ways or systems for doing something
5.		11	similar; pattern-like

* **The symbol "¶" means paragraph.** You can find the word in that paragraph.

Exercise 2

Vocabulary Fill-in Exercise: Choose the words in Exercise 1 above to fill in the blanks below.

1. Ken has been a hard worker and has done the same job at his company for several years. He decided that if he is not ____________________ soon, he will look for a different job.

2. What would you do in this ____________________? It is 1:00 a.m., and you are trying to sleep, but your neighbor is playing loud music.

3. If a child continues to cry in a store because he wants you to buy him a toy, there are several different ____________________ that you could use to resolve the problem.

4. The teacher thought that Katy copied her essay from the Internet, so she compared that essay with Katy's other essays to see if the style was ____________________.

5. I was offered a job at a company. After ____________________ the salary, the office space, and the type of work, I decided to take the job.

Exercise 3

Applied Vocabulary

1. Do you think that the method that your high school teachers used to teach you English was a good one? _______ Explain.

2. Imagine that you have a classmate in this course, and he is worried about being promoted. What advice would you give him? In other words, what should he do in order get promoted to the next level?

3. Do you think that the method that your parents used to raise you is consistent with how you would raise your own children? _______ Explain.

4. What features of this school did you analyze before you decided to enroll here?

5. Which of these scenarios would you prefer? (Choose one.)
   a) You have an interesting job, and you love to go to work every day, but you don't get a very high salary and you have only one week of vacation every year.

   b) You get a high salary and have three weeks of vacation every year, but your job is rather boring, and you don't look forward to going to work every day.

Part 3: Preparation for discussion for Unit 9

Think about your answers to these questions. You do not have to write your answers.

1. In the story about the workers in ¶ 1-4, do you think that the president should meet with the two workers separately or together? Explain your reasons.
2. Think of a conflict that you had with someone. Summarize the conflict. Did you try to find out the truth, or did you try to maintain harmony?
3. Look at the question at the end of Scenario 1 in ¶ 6. How would you respond to the teacher? Explain your reason.
4. Look at the question at the end of Scenario 2 in ¶ 7. How would you respond to the friend? Explain your reason.
5. Look at the question at the end of Scenario 3 in ¶ 8. How would you respond to your father? Explain your reason.
6. Look at Exercise 1 at the end of ¶ 8. In general, did you choose confrontation, submission or compromise? Are you surprised?
7. Look at ¶ 10. Look at the results for Scenario 1 about the teacher. What is one thing that you think is interesting or surprising about these results?
8. Look at ¶ 10. Look at the results for Scenario 2 about a best friend. What is one thing that you think is interesting or surprising about these results?
9. Look at ¶ 10. Look at the results for Scenario 3 about the father. What is one thing that you think is interesting or surprising about these results?
10. Do you have feelings similar to or different from the German students about submitting to a friend but confronting your father?

❖ For "Small-group Discussion" questions in the form of Students A, B, and C, see *Supplementary Activities*, or download it free from www.ProLinguaAssociates.com.

❖ For "Whole-class Discussion" techniques and a suggested procedure, see the *Supplementary Activities*, or download it free from www.prolinguaassociates.com.

❖ For "Applied Outside-class Interactions/Observations," see the *Supplementary Activities*, or download it free from www.prolinguaassociates.com.

Part 4: Reflection paper:

Tell what was new to you or what you learned from the source.

A common type of writing assignment in academic courses is a reflection paper. In this type of assignment, you show that you understood a reading passage by responding to it. You can do this by connecting the ideas in the passage either to your own experiences and observations, or to information that you have recently learned. Another type of reflection response is to explain how the ideas in a passage might be applied to other situations. Or you might agree or disagree with the ideas in a passage.

For this assignment, you will write a reflection paper in which you explain what was new information to you in the passage or you discuss what you learned from it. As with many reflection papers, you will start by summarizing the passage itself. Then, you will explain what was new to you by using the expressions in the box below.

Expressions for explaining what was new to you or what you learned

- ◆ I found some new information from this passage.
- ◆ Something that I learned from this passage was that…
- ◆ There is some new information for me in this passage.
- ◆ From this passage, I learned that …
- ◆ Before reading this passage, I hadn't realized that …
- ◆ I now understand that …
- ◆ One piece of new information for me was that…

Exercise 1: Re-read Unit 10.3, paragraphs 4-8, about modesty and bragging.

Exercise 2

In this exercise, you will read a sample reflection paper. In it, you will find a summary of the passage, followed by the writer's explanation of what was new or what the writer learned from it.

Directions: Fill in the blanks with the word from the box.

- ◆ how unique and important
- ◆ can speak modestly
- ◆ nobody in
- ◆ boasting
- ◆ passage explained
- ◆ strongly believed
- ◆ get the respect

Reflection Paper

(Summary of the passage)

The section, "Talents: modesty vs. bragging," tells about an experience that an American (individualist) professor had when he gave a lecture at a university in Asia. The professor ______________________________ that his lecture would be very interesting, and he tried to share his excitement with the audience. He prepared the audience by telling them ______________________________________ his research was. Unfortunately, to the audience, it appeared that the professor was _____________, which they did not like. As a result, when the time came for questions and answers and to have a discussion, _____________ the audience said anything. The author of the ______________________________ that in the professor's (individualist) culture, a speaker needs to tell the audience personal information that is positive in order to _________________________ of the audience. On the other hand, a collectivist speaker would expect his or her support group members to tell positive information about the speaker, so the speaker ______________________________ about himself or herself.

◆ realize	◆ piece of information	◆ I like	◆ reading this
◆ understand that	◆ Now I understand	◆ else that	◆ For example, one

(Reflection: Explain what was new or what was learned from it.)

Before ____________________ section, I hadn't realized how important it is for individualists to "brag" about themselves. ______________________________ that if they don't tell some good things about themselves, nobody will know it. I am from a collectivist culture, and it surprised me to hear my American friend tell me that he is good at fixing computers and even cooking. I used to have the impression that he was bragging, but now I ______ that he wants me to know in case I need his help.

Something ______________________ I learned from the article is how important support groups are for collectivists. In my culture, I usually hear people say how weak they are in certain skills. ______________________________________ of my friends had lived in Canada for five years as a child, and now speaks fluent English. However, whenever someone tells her how well she speaks English, she denies it and says that she is afraid that people don't really understand her. ________________ this. Because I am really not very good in English, I feel more comfortable when I am around her because I don't feel as if she thinks that she is smarter than me. In the passage, the author says that collectivists have a support group, who will tell the positive things about their members. I realize that I do this for that friend of mine. I always tell people how good she is at speaking English.

Finally, another ________________________________ that was new to me was how a collectivist's modesty can confuse an individualist. The author gives the example of a husband who said that his wife's cooking is poor. I hear this type of comment often in my country, but I don't believe the husband. However, now I ______________ an individualist might believe it and get a bad impression of the wife. I realize that when I apply to an American university next month, I will need to directly describe my strong points.

Exercise 3

1) Choose one of the Passages listed under the box.

2) Write a reflection paper. It should have two parts:

- ◆ A summary of the passage
- ◆ Your reflection describing what was new to you or that you learned. Try to use the expressions in the box below.

Expressions for explaining what was new to you or what you learned

- I found some new information from this passage.
- Something that I learned from this passage was ...
- There is some new information for me in this passage.
- From this passage, I learned that ...
- Before reading this passage, I hadn't realized that ...
- Now I understand that ...
- One piece of new information for me was ...

Passages

- ◆ In Unit 4, Conformity: advantages of fitting in, use ¶ 2.
- ◆ In Unit 5, re-read 5.1 Tight and loose cultures: advantages and disadvantages of strict rules of behavior.
- ◆ In Unit 6, re-read 6.2 Complimenting: A technique for joining a new group.
- ◆ In Unit 7, re-read 7.1 Context: a lot or little common background.
- ◆ In Unit 7, re-read 7.2 Non-verbal cues: speaking directly or indirectly.

Part 5: Preview for Unit 10

Directions: Answer these questions.

1. When do you smile? (Choose all that apply.)
   a) When I am happy
   b) When I am embarrassed
   c) When I am confused
   d) When I am upset

2. Imagine that you have this conversation with a classmate, Tom.

   You: I heard that our test next week is going to be hard.
   Tom: Yes, I heard that too.
   You: Some of us are planning to meet this evening to study together. Do you want to join us?
   Tom: Hummmm. (silence for 15 seconds)

   Question: What do you think is the reason for Tom's silence?
   a) He probably doesn't want to study with us.
   b) He's probably shy.
   c) He's probably thinking deeply about my idea.
   d) He probably doesn't understand my question.

3. In your culture, which of these relationships is most important?
   a) parent-child
   b) husband-wife
   c) other: ________________________

Unit 10

10.1 Smile

Happiness, embarrassment, and other emotions

Reading

[1] Surprisingly, a smile can cause misunderstandings among people from different cultures. For a Westerner (an individualist), a smile indicates a positive and friendly mood. It is not used when one feels upset or frustrated. However, in Thailand (a collectivist culture) people smile not only to show friendliness but also to hide embarrassment or anger, to avoid a conflict, or to conceal resentment or envy. When they smile in frustrating situations, others get the impression that everything is still fine. This can be confusing to an individualist who is visiting Thailand.

For example, an American woman who was living in Thailand had a maid. One day, the maid accidentally broke an expensive plate and then smiled. The American woman became upset because she thought the Thai maid considered it funny that the plate broke. However, a Thai person would understand that the maid's smile indicated that she was hiding her distress (Boesch, 1994).

10.2 Silence

Showing strength or rejection

[2] As we saw in Unit 7, when people from a high-context culture interact with those from a low-context one, misunderstandings can occur. In high-context cultures, the situation is important, and people often use non-verbal signals, such as remaining silent, breathing deeply or hesitating, to express their true thoughts. By not sharing their opinions directly,

they are able to maintain harmony within their group. In low-context cultures, the words themselves are of great importance, and people are expected to express their ideas directly. Generally speaking, collectivists tend to be from high-context cultures, and individualists tend to be from low-context ones, and when they interact, they might misunderstand each other.

3 Silence, for example, can have different meanings in different cultures. People from high-context (collectivist) cultures sometimes use silence, rather than make a comment that might cause an embarrassment or conflict. It can also give the impression that someone is seriously thinking about what the other person has said (or done). Also, some collectivists believe that saying too much might cause confusion. Silence can even show that someone is being strong. However, people from low-context (individualist) cultures often view silence negatively because they expect an immediate response after making a comment or request. They think that if someone is silent, it means that the other person: 1) does not want to have a conversation, 2) is shy, 3) lacks verbal skills, or 4) is indicating disagreement or rejection. For a collectivist, responding too quickly after someone has made a comment or request shows that the listener is not giving enough thought or consideration to the speaker's idea. This difference in attitude toward silence can be a potential problem, especially for collectivist students who attend classes in individualist countries (DeCapau and Wintergerst, 2004).

10.3 Talents

Modesty vs. bragging

4 Brislin (2001) tells this story about an American university professor, Dr. Folk, who was invited to give some lectures at a university in Asia. He was excited to share some research that he had conducted, which he felt was very interesting. He started his lecture by saying, "This is a unique study in two ways." Then he explained how the method that he had used in his research was different from other methods and how the results of his research would be very important for future research. As he was giving his lecture, he was sure that the audience would share his enthusiasm and would, at the end of his lecture, want to have a lively discussion about it. However, surprisingly, nobody asked him any questions! He felt very disappointed and confused.

5 Why didn't this Asian audience have a positive reaction to Dr. Folk? It appears they felt that he was bragging, and this made them upset. According to Brislin, their reaction is rooted in a cultural difference between collectivists and individualists. In collectivist societies, a speaker has a support group who will encourage them to give speeches and will share with the audience impressive aspects of the speaker's life, work and character so that the speaker can remain modest. For example, the speaker might say, "Thank you for taking the trouble to come to this lecture. I hope I will be able to share with you some new insights in order to make your trouble worthwhile."

6 In individualist cultures, a person like Dr. Folk often does not have such a support group who will praise his work before he gives a lecture. Thus, if he wants to be respected by the audience, he needs to speak directly and enthusiastically about his own accomplishments and explain why his research is unique and important.

7 A reverse misunderstanding can happen when a collectivist speaks modestly to an individualist. If a collectivist says to an individualist, "My son is not very intelligent," or "I'm not a very good worker," it could present a bad impression of the speaker. Imagine that a collectivist worker is applying for a job and the boss is an individualist. If the worker says, "I do not have very good skills," the boss would probably decide not to hire him.

8 Brislin gives another example of how speaking modestly could cause a problem. Let's say that a collectivist man is married to an individualist woman. They are planning to have a dinner party with some friends, so the wife spends all day cooking. After the guests arrive and as they are about to eat dinner, the collectivist husband says, "Please excuse this poorly-prepared meal. My wife is not a very good cook." This comment could be upsetting to the individualist wife who takes pride in her cooking skills. If the party takes place in a collectivist culture, the guests would probably understand that the husband is proud of his wife's cooking talents.

Part 1: Study guide for Unit 10

1. Jinji is from an Asian (i.e., a collectivist) country. Sandy is from Canada (an individualist country). Sandy asks Jinji if she wants to share an apartment. Jinji doesn't say anything but just smiles. What can we imagine about Jinji?

   a) Jinji smiled because she thought that it was a funny idea.
   b) Jinji is happy about Sandy's suggestion that they share an apartment.
   c) Jinji probably does not want to share an apartment with Sandy.

2. In the story in Question 1 (above), what will Sandy probably think about Jinji?

   a) Sandy will probably think that Jinji likes the idea and wants to share the apartment.
   b) Sandy will probably think that Jinji does not like the idea because she is smiling.
   c) Sandy will probably think that Jinji is thinking about a joke that she heard.

3. In ¶ 1, in the third sentence, it says that some people smile "to conceal resentment or envy." Which of these is an example of that? Imagine that Brad goes to a party. (Choose all that apply.)

   a) He sees his former girlfriend, whom he still loves, holding hands with his best friend. Brad smiles.
   b) The hostess of the party, Tina, tells him that she is happy that he came. Brad smiles.
   c) He is talking with his friend, Travis. Travis tells Brad that he has been accepted to a famous university that had already rejected Brad's application. Brad smiles.
   d) Ken tells everyone a funny joke. Brad smiles.

4. In ¶ 1, when the maid broke the plate, her reaction was to smile because ___.

   a) she thought it was funny
   b) she didn't think it was a serious mistake
   c) she felt upset
   d) she had a plan to hide the plate

5. This question is about ¶2. Imagine that I am at my job. My co-worker, Anna, needs to leave the office and drive to meet with a customer, but it is raining. Anna and I are standing near the door looking outside.

Question: In which of these situations did I use context to know what Anna wanted?

Situation A

Anna sticks her hand out the door and feels the rain on it. Then she just looks out the door with a worried look on her face. I understand that Anna would like to borrow my umbrella.

Situation B

Anna looks at the rain and says to me, "Would you mind if I borrow your umbrella?" I understand that Anna would like to borrow my umbrella.

6. ¶ 3-4, is about the American professor's lecture at the Asian university. The audience didn't ask him questions or discuss his lecture because ___.

   a) they were too shy to participate
   b) the information in his lecture was not interesting or new to them
   c) he didn't speak in their language, so they didn't understand very well
   d) they didn't like his self-important and overly-confident attitude about himself

7. Read the situations below, and fill in the blanks with ***probably will respect*** or ***might not respect***.

Situation 1

A collectivist speaker says to a collectivist audience, "My lecture might not be very interesting to you."

◆ The audience ______________________________ the speaker.

Situation 2

A collectivist speaker says to an individualist audience, "My lecture might not be interesting to you."

◆ The audience ______________________________ the speaker.

Situation 3

An individualist speaker says to a collectivist audience, "I have some very interesting information in my lecture."

◆ The audience ______________________________ the speaker.

Situation 4

An individualist speaker says to an individualist audience, "I have some very interesting information in my lecture."

◆ The audience ______________________________ the speaker.

8. This question is about ¶ 7-8. Let's say that Sara's son is an excellent piano player. If Sara tells you, "My son is a weak piano player. When he plays, sometimes it hurts my ears." Sara is probably _____.

   a) a collectivist
   b) an individualist

9. Let's say I am an individualist, and Sara and her son are my friends. After Sara says, "My son is a weak piano player. When he plays, sometimes it hurts my ears," I might think that _____.

   a) her son is actually a very good piano player
   b) her son is actually not a very good piano player

10. Write one clarification question about a word, sentence, or idea that you do not understand in this unit. (If you understand everything, pretend that you don't.)

Part 2: Academic Vocabulary for Unit 10

Exercise 1

Words from context: Look at the paragraphs listed in the middle column of the chart below to find the words that have the meanings in the column on the right.

	Word	¶ *	Find the word that means . . .
1.		2	happen
2.		3	possible
3.		5	parts of something, e.g., parts of a plan, an idea, a problem, etc.
4.		5	clear understanding of something that is complicated
5.		7	humbly; if you do something modestly, you do not talk in a proud way about your skills

* **The symbol "¶" means paragraph.** You can find the word in that paragraph.

Exercise 2

Vocabulary Fill-in Exercise: Choose the words in Exercise 1 above to fill in the blanks below.

1. The best ________________ of Tom's apartment is the beautiful view that he sees from his windows.

2. I never knew that Amy was the best student when she was in college because she always spoke ____________ about her grades.

3. If young people use a lot of slang when they talk to older people, a communication breakdown might ______________ .

4. I realized that there was a __________________ problem with my new roommate when he asked me if he could borrow some money immediately after I met him.

5. Brian was having problems training his dog. One day, he read an article which said that we shouldn't let our dog sleep in our beds with us. That article gave Brian a good ___________________ into his problem.

Exercise 3: Applied Vocabulary

1. What is a potential problem someone can have from being very rich?

2. Let's say that your friend told you, "My cell phone recently stopped working. Would you have any insights into what the problem might be?" What would you say?

3. Which of our classmates do you think speaks modestly?

4. What is a positive aspect of married life?

5. In the world, what is something that has happened that shows us that global warming might be occurring?

Part 3: Preparation for discussion for Unit 10

Think about your answers to these questions. You do not have to write your answers.

1. Do you sometimes smile to avoid a conflict, to hide embarrassment, or to hide anger? Give an example of when you have done this.

2. Are you sometimes confused when you see people smile? Give an example.

3. Do you sometimes feel uncomfortable if someone is silent or if someone isn't silent? Give an example.

4. In your culture, which is more common: a speaker says that his speech will be unique and interesting, or a speaker says that his speech might not be very good?

5. Which style of speaker do you prefer? Explain.

6. Do your family members speak modestly about each other? For example, would your father say that your mother is not a good cook? Would your parents tell people that you are not a good student? How would these make you feel?

> ❖ For "Small-group Discussion" questions in the form of Students A, B, and C, see ***Supplementary Activities***, or download it free from www.ProLinguaAssociates.com.

> ❖ For "Whole-class Discussion" techniques and a suggested procedure, see the ***Supplementary Activities***, or download it free from www.prolinguaassociates.com.

> ❖ For "Applied Outside-class Interactions/Observations," see the ***Supplementary Activities***, or download it free from www.prolinguaassociates.com.

Part 4: A technique for writing a reflection paper

Tell what is important or significant about the source information.

As mentioned in Unit 9, a common type of writing assignment in academic courses is a reflection paper. For this assignment, you will write a reflection paper in which you explain what was important or significant about the information in the source. As with many reflection papers, you will start by summarizing the passage. Then, you will explain what was important or significant by using the expressions in the box below.

Expressions for explaining what is important or significant
◆ This information is significant in several ways.
◆ What is important about this is …
◆ This is important information.
◆ I think that it is significant that …
◆ There are some important points that we learned from this.
◆ Another important point is that…

Exercise 1

Re-read Unit 4, paragraphs 6 & 7, about the "conformity" experiments.

Exercise 2

In this exercise, you will read a sample reflection paper. In it, you will find a summary of the passage followed by the writer's explanation of what is important or significant about the information.

Directions: Fill in the blanks with the words in the box.

• pressure from	• tried to identify	• On top of that
• experiment involved	• learned that	• purposefully

(Summary of the passage)

In the section titled "Conformity: advantages of fitting in," the author describes an experiment about conformity. The ______________________________ a subject and four confederates, who were all Americans. There were also two charts; one chart had a line on it, and the other chart had three lines on it. The subject and confederates looked at the two charts and ____________________ which line in the second chart matched the one line in the first chart. The confederates, who were secretly working with the researcher, Asch, ____________________ identified the wrong line in order to see if the subject would agree with them. Surprisingly, 33% of the time, the subjects conformed to what the confederates had said. Asch also conducted this experiment with a Japanese subject and American confederates. In these situations, the subjects only conformed 20% of the time. ____________________, 34% of the time, the Japanese subject purposefully chose the wrong line after the American confederates had chosen the correct line! We ____________________ ________ this might be because the Americans were not in-group members for the Japanese subjects, so the Japanese subjects made an anti-conformity choice because they did not want to respond to the ____________________ an out-group.

◆ Another important point	◆ historical	◆ me, this shows
◆ together	◆ significant in several	◆ wrong is right simply
◆ also significant	◆ responded by saying	◆ in fact, wrong

(Reflection: Explain what is important or significant about the information.)

This information is ________________________________ ways. First, I think that it is significant that a third of the subjects would purposefully make a mistake in order to conform to others. To ________________________ that the education system is not doing a good job. An educated person should have confidence and shouldn't say something is correct if it is ______________________, just because other people made a certain choice. My parents often tried to teach me this. When I was 15, my parents refused to let me get a tattoo. I complained and tried to convince them by saying that all my friends were allowed to get one. My mother ________________________, "Would you jump in the ocean if all your friends did?"

________________________________ is that this research shows us how people can be easily misled. We can find many ________________ examples of groups of people and even countries that have done terrible things, and we wonder why they were able to do them. One reason is because people are willing to say that something ______________________ because many other people are saying it.

I think that it is ______________________ that a collectivist person might not conform to a group even if the group is doing the right thing just because the collectivist does not want to be pressured by out-group members. This could help us understand why some groups are not able to work ______________________.

Exercise 3

1) Choose one of the Passages listed under the box.

2) Write a reflection paper. It should have two parts:

- ◆ A summary of the passage
- ◆ Your reflection describing what is significant or important about the information in the passage. Try to use the expressions in the box below.

Expressions for explaining what is important or significant

- ◆ This information is significant in several ways.
- ◆ What is important about this is that…
- ◆ This is important information.
- ◆ I think that it is significant that …
- ◆ There are some important points that we learned from this.
- ◆ Another important point is that…

Passages

- ◆ In Unit 2, use 2.2, Collectivism and individualism: group-oriented vs. self-oriented
- ◆ In Unit 3, re-read 3.4, In-groups: close vs. casual relationships
- ◆ In Unit 5, re-read 5.1, Tight and loose cultures: advantages and disadvantages of strict rules of behavior
- ◆ In Unit 6, re-read 6.1, Forming in-groups: needing or not needing party skills
- ◆ In Unit 8, re-read 8.1, Sending messages: how it is said rather than what is said

Part 5: Preview for Unit 11

1. Imagine that your neighbor's son is very good in math. How would you explain how he got his ability? (Choose one.)

   a. He probably worked hard.
   b. He probably has naturally good ability.

2. A boy and a girl are in the same class in college. When they are in the same group, he looks at her with close attention while she is talking and smiles. If they leave the building together, he opens the door for her. What do you think about this boy?

   a. He likes the girl and would like her to be his girlfriend.
   b. He is just being polite.

Section 3

How collectivists' and individualists' perceptions are different

1 In Sections 1 and 2, we read about the different norms that collectivists and individualists have and about their different styles of interacting. In this section, we will explore why collectivists and individualists have different perceptions. For example, in some cultures, a smile can indicate emotions besides happiness. We will look at relationships and answer the question: Which relationships are most important in different cultures? Also, we will read about how different cultures feel about giving opinions, how they view time, what they think the reasons are for success and failure, and what the most important characteristics are in a marriage partner.

Unit 11

11.1 Attribution

Explanation for personal success or failure

Reading

2 Imagine that you are sitting at a table in a library, and you are reading a magazine. You look up from what you are reading at the same moment that a stranger who is sitting at the next table looks up and catches your eye. The stranger smiles at you briefly. Why did the stranger smile at you? Was it because that person wanted to become your friend? Was it because the social norm is to smile at someone in order to show politeness? Was it because that person thought that you were wearing a funny-looking shirt?

[3] Now, let's say that the opposite happens. When you catch the eye of the stranger, you smile first. Why did you smile?

[4] The reason why you think that someone acted (or you acted) in a certain manner is called attribution. Perhaps you think the stranger smiled at you because that person thought that you were attractive. In this case, you attributed the stranger's smile to their attraction to you. If you think you smiled at the stranger because it was the social norm of politeness, then you attributed your action to the social norm (Koenig and Dean, 2011).

[5] Attributions can cause confusion between collectivists and individualists. An individualist may just be following the social norm for politeness, but a collectivist may attribute the individualist's action to something else. As discussed in Unit 6, individualists develop "party skills" and other techniques that they use when they meet new people; they also use these to develop new relationships. They will often sound very enthusiastic when talking to someone whom they have just met because they consider it to be polite, and they believe that it will make them appear more interesting, which, in turn, will leave a positive impression in the other person's memory. On the other hand, collectivists, who tend to interact mainly with their in-group members, do not need to develop this style of enthusiastic interaction. For them, if someone sounds enthusiastic about something that they had said, they will think that, instead of just being polite, that person actually has a personal interest in them (Brislin, 1994). The following story demonstrates this kind of misunderstanding.

[6] Let's take Tamako, an Asian student; she was studying at an American university. During the orientation for first-year students, she met Jack, an American who came from a southern state in the U.S. As with most young people from that part of the U. S., Jack had been taught especially polite manners, particularly when interacting with women, and as a result, during the orientation, he treated Tamako with his usual level of politeness. For example, whenever they had a conversation, he always smiled and looked at her attentively. Also, during the orientation, Jack took the new students on a tour of the campus. When they were about to enter a building, Jack held the door open for Tamako. One time, as they were about to cross a busy intersection of a street, he gently held her elbow to guide her. Tamako was excited about making this new friend and, that evening, sent an email to her friends in Japan telling them that she had an American boyfriend (Cushner and Brislin, 1996).

7 Brislin and Cushner explain the misunderstanding that Tamako had. In most Asian countries, casual interactions and touching between people of the opposite sex is unusual unless the two people are attracted to each other. Thus, Tamako attributed Jack's actions, e.g., holding her elbow, opening doors, and smiling at her, as indications that he wanted to be a close friend. For Jack, those actions were just good manners in general and had no special meaning; they were merely the social norms for politeness.

8 There are two types of attribution. One is called internal attribution, in which the cause of the action is connected to someone's personality, mood, attitude, ability or effort. For example, if you think the reason why a stranger smiled at you was because of your attractiveness, this would be an internal attribution. The second type is called external attribution, in which the cause of the behavior is connected to something in the environment, for example, luck or social norms. If you think the stranger smiled at you because that person thought your shirt looked funny, it means that you were making an external attribution.

9 One day, a teacher returned a test to a group of students. The students had different reasons for why they had done well or poorly:

Amy: I think I got a good grade because I tried very hard.
Ken: I think I got a good grade because the test was easy.
Mari: I think I got a bad grade because I don't have good skills.
Jim: I think I got a bad grade because the teacher didn't teach us very well.

10 These students all attributed their grades to either their internal or external explanations. An internal explanation would indicate that it was due to a personal quality (I did well because I tried hard; or I did poorly because I don't have good skills), and an external explanation would suggest that a result happened because of a situation or an environmental factor (I did well because the test was easy; or I didn't do well because the teacher didn't teach us very well).

11 Some researchers (Holloway, Kashiwagi, Hess, and Azuma, 1986) theorized that attribution could partially explain why Asian students perform better in math than American students do. Studies show that the difference in achievement is not connected to the content that is taught to students in the different places. It is true that students in many Asian countries have more class-days and that they spend a greater percentage of class time studying math. However, Holloway et al. (1986) found another difference between Asian and Americans that could also be a factor.

[12] In previous studies, researchers asked people to complete this sentence: "He is successful because of ___ ." They found that 72% of the Japanese chose "his effort" while only 1% said "his ability." In the study by Holloway et al. (1985), the researchers asked Japanese and American mothers to rate their children's performance in math. The mothers who said that their children were doing average or poor work were asked to choose one of these reasons:

___ My child lacks ability in math.
___ My child does not study hard in math.
___ My child does not have good instruction in school.
___ My child is unlucky in math.
___ Math is difficult.

[13] Japanese mothers most often chose "My child does not study hard" as the reason for their child poor performance in math. They rarely blamed other factors. Although American mothers also attributed lack of effort to their child's poor results, they were more likely than the Japanese mothers to assign blame to the child's instructors or to the school.

[14] Similar studies were conducted in Taiwan and Hong Kong. In the Taiwanese study, Chinese parents of primary school children were more apt to say that their children were successful due to their hard work, whereas American parents explained their children's success as innate (i.e., natural) ability. In the Hong Kong study, Chinese university students were asked to explain their academic performance. Over 80% chose "effort" as the explanation (Stevenson and Lee, 1990). The researchers believe that these different attitudes could partially explain the reason why Asian students outperform their American counterparts. If people feel that they just need to work harder in order to be successful, they tend to be more motivated to increase their effort compared to a person who believes that they just do not have the natural ability to improve. These latter ones are more apt to feel resignation; in other words, they believe that no matter how hard they work, they will still be a failure.

[15] Researchers conducted a study with first-grade students in Asia and America. They wanted to see how much time the students would spend working on a math problem that would be impossible for first graders to solve – before they gave up. The American students tried to solve the problem for less than 30 seconds on average. Then, they stopped and told the researchers that they couldn't solve it because they hadn't studied that yet. Every Asian student, on the other hand, worked on the impossible math problem for a whole hour. They didn't stop until the researchers told them to. In sum, ". . . if struggle indicates weakness to you – for example a lack of intelligence – it makes you feel bad, so you're less likely to put up with it. But if struggle indicates strength – the ability to face down challenge – you are much more willing to accept it" (Spiegel, 2012).

11.2 Effort vs. ability

Cause of misunderstanding

16 As discussed above, Asians tend to attribute their success or failure to the effort they made, whereas Americans think that innate ability plays a very important role. This difference in viewpoint about effort and ability can cause misunderstandings between collectivists and individualists.

17 Jay, a student from Asia who is studying at a college in the U.S., received a failing grade for one of his courses. He is hoping that he can convince his American teacher to change his grade. He tells the teacher that he had studied very hard during the course and even stayed up all night re-reading the textbook before quizzes. He asks the teacher to give him a passing grade because of the great effort that he had made. This Asian proverb could explain Jay's perspective: "Enough shovels of earth—a mountain. Enough pails of water—a river." In other words, if people make a great effort, there will be a positive result. A study found that Chinese and Japanese students credited their success to studying hard more often than American students did. In another study, students in Hong Kong stated that the most important cause of success in school and at a job is effort (Koenig and Dean, 2011).

18 Most American teachers would probably compliment Jay on his good effort but would explain that, in order to pass the course, students need to demonstrate that they have mastered the coursework and/or that they have attained the level of ability to succeed in the next level of coursework. For example, an ESL student from Asia works very hard to improve his writing skills and, therefore, feels that he deserves to be promoted to the next level. Nevertheless, if his skills are not yet high enough for him to be successful in the next level, the instructor will probably not pass him until he has developed those skills.

Part 1: Study guide for Unit 11

Questions

1. In ¶ 4, attribution means that ___.
   a) you think you know the reason for someone's actions
   b) someone told you the reason for someone's actions
   c) you know the reason for someone's actions

2. According to ¶ 4, why did the stranger smile at you?
   a) It was because that person wanted to be your friend.
   b) It was because that person was being polite.
   c) We don't know the exact reason.

3. In the story in ¶ 6, what are four things that Jack did that made Tamako think that he wanted to be her boyfriend? (Choose all that apply.)
   a) He smiled at her.
   b) He asked her for her telephone number.
   c) He looked interested in what she said during their conversations.
   d) He gave her his chair to sit on since there were not enough.
   e) He opened a door for her.
   f) He touched her elbow when they were walking across a street.
   g) He winked at her.

4. Why was Jack so friendly to Tamako?
   a) His family taught him to be polite.
   b) He wanted to ask Tamako for a date.
   c) His job was to help new students.

5. What did Tamako attribute Jack's actions to?
   a) She attributed them to his social norms, i.e., his good manners.
   b) She attributed them to his interest in her and his desire to have a date with her.
   c) She attributed them to how American men treat women.

6. ¶s 8-10 discuss attributions. In the blanks, write ***internal*** or ***external*** about attributions.
   a) ____________________ attribution: The reason why I had a car accident was because of the rain and wet conditions of the road.

b) ____________________ attribution: The reason why I had a car accident was because I was thinking about my work and wasn't paying attention to my driving.

c) ____________________ attribution: The reason why we lost the basketball game was because we had not practiced enough.

d) ____________________ attribution: The reason why we lost our basketball game was because the other team's players were taller than us.

e) ____________________ attribution: The reason why I have a lot of money is because my grandfather died, and I inherited it.

f) ____________________ attribution: The reason why I have a lot of money is because I worked 60 hours a week for five years and saved 50% of my salary.

7. According to ¶ 13, if Japanese students didn't do well on a math test, their mothers were apt to say that the reason was ___. (Choose all that apply.)
   a) their teacher or school did not do a good job
   b) their children did not work hard enough
   c) their children have poor math skills

8. According to ¶ 13, if American students didn't do well on a math test, their mothers were apt to say that the reason was ___. (Choose all that apply.)
   a) their teacher or school did not do a good job
   b) their children did not work hard enough
   c) their children have poor math skills

9. According to ¶ 14, researchers believe that one reason why Chinese perform better than Americans is because ___. (Choose all that apply.)
   a) Asian textbooks are better
   b) Asian instructors use better methods of teaching
   c) Asians believe that success comes from working hard
   d) Asians have more school days each year
   e) Asians have more natural ability

10. According to ¶ 14, which of these statements will motivate students more?
   a) If you work hard, you will be successful.
   b) If you have a natural ability, you will be successful.

11. This is about the quote at the end of ¶ 15. Answer the questions below. Fill in the blanks with ***Asian students*** or ***American students***.

    a) ______________________ feel that if you struggle to solve something, it shows that you are not very intelligent.

    b) ______________________ feel that if you struggle to solve something, it shows that you are strong.

12. This is about ¶ 16. Read the statements below and decide who probably said them. Fill in the blanks with ***Asians*** or ***Americans***.

    a) The reason why I was able to fix my computer is because I took computer science courses for two years and spent about 10 hours a day working with them. ______________________

    b) The reason why I was able to fix my computer is because I have a natural understanding about how computers work. Even as a child, I understood them.
    ____

13. This item is about ¶ 17-18. Imagine that Trish, a student in an American college class, gets a passing grade. Which of these are probably the reasons? (Choose all that apply.)

    a) She wrote a 30-page report, but her classmates wrote only 20 pages.
    b) She wrote only a 15-page report, but in the report she showed that she had understood the textbook and the instructor's lectures.
    c) She got the highest grades in the class on the two tests.
    d) She stayed up studying until 2:00 a.m. translating difficult parts of the textbook, she came to class early every day, and she asked her instructors a lot of questions.

14. Write one clarification question about a word, sentence, or idea that you do not understand in this unit. (If you understand everything, pretend that you don't.)

Part 2: Academic Vocabulary Development Unit 11

Exercise 1

Words from context: Look at the paragraphs listed in the middle column of the chart below to find the words that have the meanings in the column on the right.

	Word	¶ *	Find the word that means . . .
1.		4	believed that something was caused by something else
2.		10	one of several things that can cause something
3.		14	an ability or characteristic that a person has at birth
4.		17	believed that someone or something was successful for some reason(s)
5.		18	gained; achieved; got

* **The symbol "¶" means paragraph.** You can find the word in that paragraph.

Exercise 2

Vocabulary Fill-in Exercise: Choose the words in Exercise 1 above to fill in the blanks below.

1. In general, children have an ________________ ability to learn languages.
2. Alex's financial situation is bad. He has a low income and does not save much money. Perhaps the biggest ______________________ is that he likes to gamble and usually loses.
3. Jay had a serious car accident, but he was not hurt. He ______________________ the car's air bags with saving his life.
4. Bill Gates ____________________ his reputation as a brilliant businessman through his management of his company, Microsoft.
5. I asked Ben how he gained so much weight. He ______________________ it to all the junk food that he ate.

Exercise 3

Applied Vocabulary

1. You can speak English. Do you attribute your ability mostly to your parents, teachers, or your natural ability?

2. Think about something that you are good at doing, e.g., a sport, a language, or a skill. Who would you credit with helping you develop this ability?

3. Think about a pet that you have (or had) or an animal that you know about. What is an innate ability that it seems (or seemed) to have?

4. Imagine that you attained popularity as a movie star and that now you are famous. What is one problem that you could have as a result of your fame?

5. What is one of the most important factors for a person's success in learning English?

Part 3: Preparation for discussion of Unit 11

Think about your answers to these questions. You do not have to write your answers.

1. Imagine that you are sitting at a table in a library reading a magazine. You look up from your magazine at the same time that a stranger sitting at the table looks up and catches your eye. The stranger smiles at you briefly. Why do you think that the stranger smiled at you?

2. In the story about Jack and Tamako, were you surprised that Tamako thought that Jack was her boyfriend? Explain.

3. Think about a test in which you did not do well. Tell what the test was. Why did you not do well? Are you making an internal or external attribution?

4. Which of these factors do you feel is the reason why most students are successful in school: hard work or ability? Give some examples.

5. Imagine that I am Jay (in ¶ 17) and you are his American instructor. What would you say to me about my grade?

6. If you were Jay's instructor, would you give Jay a passing grade? Explain.

7. For our class, if a student works very hard and does all the assignments but doesn't do good work, should that student pass?

❖ For "Small-group Discussion" questions in the form of Students A, B, and C, see ***Supplementary Activities***, or download it free from www.ProLinguaAssociates.com.

❖ For "Whole-class Discussion" techniques and a suggested procedure, see the ***Supplementary Activities***, or download it free from www.prolinguaassociates.com.

❖ For "Applied Outside-class Interactions/Observations," see the ***Supplementary Activities***, or download it free from www.prolinguaassociates.com.

Part 4: Applying techniques for writing a reflection paper

◆ *Tell what is new to you or what you learned.*

◆ *Tell what was significant or important.*

In Units 9 and 10, we practiced techniques for writing reflection papers. In this unit, you will look at a model reflection in which all the techniques are applied, and then you will write a reflection paper that uses that style.

Expressions for explaining what is important or significant

- ◆ This information is significant in several ways.
- ◆ What is important about this is that...
- ◆ This is important information.
- ◆ I think that it is significant that ...
- ◆ There are some important points that we learned from this.
- ◆ Another important point is that...

Expressions for introducing what was new to you or what you learned

- ◆ I found some new information from this passage.
- ◆ Something that I learned from this passage was that...
- ◆ There is some new information for me in this passage.
- ◆ From this passage, I learned that ...
- ◆ Before reading this passage, I hadn't realized that ...
- ◆ I now understand that ...
- ◆ One piece of new information for me was that...

Exercise 1

Read this article about culture and time.

1 Another aspect of time is how people in various cultures view time. Some view it as exact, and others view it as approximate. If you have a friend who views time as exact, and you plan to meet each other at a coffee shop at 10:00 a.m., he will probably arrive very close to 10:00 a.m. exactly. However, if you had the same plan with a friend who views time as approximate, he might arrive between 9:45 and 10:30. Also, if that person was having a conversation with a friend, he wouldn't cut the conversation off even if he were late for an appointment (DeCapau and Wintergerst, 2004).

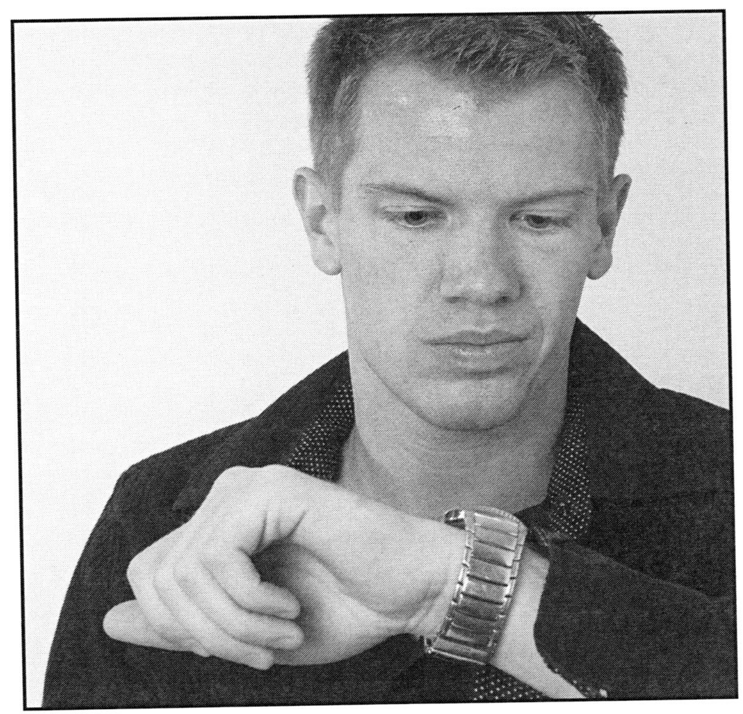

2 Researchers asked people to imagine this situation: You make plans to meet a friend at a restaurant at 6:00 p.m. If your friend does not arrive at that time, how long will you wait until you decide that your friend is not coming? Europeans and people from North America said about 15 minutes. In some less developed countries, they said one day. They said that if their friend did not come that day, they would return to the restaurant the next day to see if the friend had finally arrived (Levine & Bartlett, 1984). Interestingly, researchers found that, in Brazil, someone who often arrives late for appointments is considered to be more likeable, happy, and successful than someone who arrives on time (Smith & Bond, 1994).

3 It appears that people in different cultures even have different concepts about how fast time passes. Researchers asked people in the U.S. and Mexico to tell them when one minute had passed. They found that Mexicans tended to think that one minute had passed when actually 90 seconds had passed. In contrast, the Americans thought one minute had passed after only 48 seconds (Diaz-Guerrero 1979).

Exercise 2

In this exercise, you will read a sample reflection paper. In Part 1, you will find a summary of the passage. In Part 2, the writer explains what was important, significant, or new, or what they learned from it.

Part 1: Fill in the blanks with the words from the box.

◆ Researchers found	◆ In fact	◆ "exact" person	◆ aspect concerning
◆ authors describe	◆ contrast	◆ good chance	◆ general time

(Summary of the passage)

According to *Cultural Differences*, people in different cultures have different concepts of time. The ________________ two types of people. One type is people who view time as exact. If you have an appointment with an ________________, you can be sure that they will arrive on time. The other type is people who view time as approximate. For this type, 1:00 p.m. could mean a ________________ around 1:00 p.m. Thus, if you have an appointment with an "approximate" person, there is a ________________ that they will arrive earlier or later than the planned time.

________________ that people from Europe, the U.S., and Canada, tend to be exact types. If they have a plan to meet someone, but the other person is 15 minutes late, they will imagine that the person is not coming. In ____________, in "approximate" countries, if someone is much later than 15 minutes, the person who is waiting will think that the other person is still coming. ____________, people in Brazil tend to see many positive traits in someone who is often late.

There is a final ________________ different concepts of time. Researchers have found that a person from the U.S. will think that a minute has passed, when actually only 48 seconds had. On the other hand, a Mexican will feel that a minute takes 90 seconds to pass.

Part 2: Fill in the blanks with the words from the box.

◆ realize that ◆ understand ◆ that it is significant
◆ not serious ◆ significant because ◆ found some new
◆ important point ◆ after reading

(Reflection: Explain what was important, significant, and new, or what they learned from it.)

I ________________________ information from this passage. I used to think that if someone was late for a meeting, it was because they were impolite. Now, I _____________ they just might have a different concept of time. This is _________________________ it could affect relationships. For example, a few years ago, I lived in an Asian country that considered time as exact. One day, I had a plan to meet three friends outside a coffee shop at 3:00 p.m. At 2:55, while I was walking to the shop, I got a call on my cell phone. The three friends were at the coffee shop, and they were concerned that I hadn't arrived yet, even though it was five minutes early! I felt as though they were putting pressure on me, and I didn't like it. However, ________________________ this passage, I now ________ that it is just a part of their culture.

Another __________________________ is about how much time people think it takes for a minute to pass. If people feel that a minute has passed, when actually only 48 seconds has, it makes sense that they could feel some tension if they need to wait for someone. They will probably feel as though they have been waiting much longer than they actually have.

Finally, I think _____________________________________ that some cultures have a positive opinion of people who arrive late. I found this to be amazing because it is the opposite of how people in my culture view tardiness. For example, instructors in college tend to believe that a student who is often late for class is lazy or is _____________ about the course.

Exercise 3

1) Choose one of the Passages listed under the box.

2) Write a reflection paper. It should have two parts:

- ◆ A summary of the passage
- ◆ Your reflection describing what was important, significant, and new, or what you learned from it. Try to use the expressions below.

Expressions for explaining what is important or significant

- ◆ This information is significant in several ways.
- ◆ What is important about this is that…
- ◆ This is important information.
- ◆ I think that it is significant that …
- ◆ There are some important points that I learned from this.
- ◆ Another important point is that…

Expressions for introducing what was new to you or what you learned

- ◆ I found some new information from this passage.
- ◆ Something that I learned from this passage was …
- ◆ There is some new information for me in this passage.
- ◆ From this passage, I learned that …
- ◆ Before reading this passage, I hadn't realized that …
- ◆ Now I understand that …
- ◆ One piece of new information for me was that…

Passages

- ◆ In Unit 7, re-read 7.3, about saving face.
- ◆ In Unit 9, re-read 9. 2, about handling personal problems.
- ◆ In Unit 10, re-read 10.1 and 10.2, about smiling and silence.
- ◆ In Unit 10, re-read 10.3, about bragging and modesty.

Part 5: Preview for Unit 12

1. Imagine that you are in a store in your country, and you are paying a clerk for something. How do you give your money to the clerk?

   a) I put the money on the counter, and the clerk picks it up.
   b) I put the money in the clerk's hand.
   c) Other: ______________________

2. Fill in the blanks below with the name of a foreign country. Then choose the best answer.

   ◆ Let's say that I am studying in a library. The person at the next table comes from ______________. This person's cell phone rings, and they answer it and have a conversation, which interrupts my studying. (Choose one).

   a) I will probably think that people from ____________________ tend to be rude.
   b) I will probably think that this person is rude.

3. Let's say that I am studying in a library. The person at a table near me comes from my country. This person's cell phone rings, and they answer it and have a conversation, which interrupts my studying. (Choose one).

   a) I will probably think that people from my country tend to be rude.
   b) I will probably think that this person is rude.

Unit 12

Fundamental attribution error

Explanation for others' behavior

Reading

[1] An American student visited New York with a German student, Dieter. He noticed that anytime his German friend would pay for something, he always put the money on the counter, never in the cashier's hand. He also noticed that the cashiers sometimes looked annoyed at Dieter for not placing the money directly in their hands, especially when their hands were stretched out, ready to accept the money directly. Adding to the American's concern was the fact that the majority of the time, the cashier was black. The American interpreted this as Dieter's prejudice against touching the cashiers' hands. The American student, who was also black, knew that historically, not placing money directly in the hands of Blacks was a form of disrespect. Later, the American student went to visit Dieter in Germany and saw that everyone there placed the money on the counter and that there was even a little plastic dish to put the money on. In fact, when the American tried to give the money directly to the cashier, he was told to put it in the dish; the purpose of the dish was to make the process of counting the money easier for the cashier. In sum, the American was attributing something negative to Dieter's behavior because of his own cultural background (DeCapua and Wintergerst, 2004).

[2] If we attribute an event to something, we say that something caused the event. For example, Sara and Tom are walking on a sidewalk, and Tom slips on a patch of ice and falls down. Sara might say that the reason why Tom fell was because he was careless or clumsy. In other words, she attributed his fall to his personality (his disposition). On the other hand, if Sara herself had slipped on the ice and fell, she might blame it on the ice (the situation).

[3] By making attributions, we try to explain the behavior of others (and of ourselves). If a friend fails to meet you at a coffee shop at a time when you had planned to meet, you might attribute your friend's behavior to irresponsibility (personality / disposition) or to the fact that there was so much traffic (situation) (Matsumoto, 2000).

[4] The concept, **fundamental attribution error**, describes the tendency to do just what Sara did when she blamed Tom himself for falling, but she would blame the ice if she fell. When someone else did something wrong, we explain their behavior by saying that it was because of their personality or character, i.e., a *dispositional explanation*, rather than an explanation that is connected to the situation.

[5] Andy is a Canadian college student living in an apartment. In an apartment next to him are four Chinese students, whom he doesn't know very well. Two Canadians live on the other side of his apartment. One evening while he was trying to study, he was disturbed by a noisy party. At first, he thought the noise was coming from the Chinese students. He said to himself, "Chinese are so rude. They only care about themselves." After a few minutes, he realized that the Chinese students were not having the party; it was the Canadians! He then thought, "These apartment walls are too thin."

[6] In Andy's story above, he is exhibiting a fundamental attribution error. He believes the negative action of an out-group to be caused by *internal factors* (their personalities or other internal traits), but views his in-group's negative action to be caused by *external factors* (the environment or situation). For example, someone might look at a group of homeless people and explain their difficulties to be the result of laziness or drug addiction (internal). On the other hand, homeless people might say that the reason for their situation is that no one will help them, or that there is no affordable housing, or that there are no jobs (external). For positive actions, the reverse is true. For example, if our soccer team wins a game (a positive action), we tend to say it was because of our great skill and determination (i.e., internal—in this case, our ability / traits). However, if our opponent wins, we are likely

to say it was because they were lucky or because the referees were bad (external—in that case, the situation) (Triandis, 1994).

[7] It's not uncommon for people to hear students attribute a classmate's bad grade to low intelligence (internal), but at the same time, attribute their own bad grade to bad luck or to a teacher's choice of questions, to a poorly-designed test, to ineffective teaching, or to a noisy study environment (external).

[8] Similarly, group members will say that bad behavior by a member of their in-group was caused by an external factor (e.g., the situation), whereas good behavior was due to internal factors (e.g., the excellent characteristics in their group member's personality). On the other hand, a group will attribute bad behavior by out-group members to internal factors (e.g., the weak points in the out-group members' personality) and good behavior to external factors (e.g., the situation) (Triandis, 1994).

[9] To illustrate this, let's imagine that cats and dogs can talk and that they have in-group and out-group members. (For dogs, all other dogs are in their in-group and all cats are in their out-group, and vice versa.) One day, a dog named Spike does something bad; he bites a man. If we ask other dogs (Spike's in-group) why Spike bit the man, they would say that it was because the man was mean to Spike; he tried to steal Spike's food. (This would be an external factor and thus not Spike's fault). If we asked some cats (Spike's out-group) why Spike bit the man, the cats would say it was because Spike has a bad temper, which causes him to attack people for no good reason. (This would be an internal factor and thus Spike's fault.) On the other hand, let's say that Spike helps a blind person walk across a busy street. The other dogs would say that Spike did that because he is kind and likes to help people. (This would be an internal factor, thanks to Spike's good character.) The cats would say that Spike helped the blind man because his owner always rewards Spike with a treat when he helps someone. (This would be an external factor and did not show that Spike had a good character).

[10] Smith and Bond discussed a study of Hindus and Muslims in India. Researchers described some situations to 30 Hindu clerks. Some of the situations were desirable (e.g., a shopkeeper was generous with a customer), and some were undesirable (e.g., a shopkeeper cheated a customer). In some situations, the shopkeeper was an in-group (Hindu) and in others, he was an out-group (Muslim). They then asked the clerks to explain the shopkeepers' motives in the various situations. In desirable situations, the clerks tended to say that positive actions by in-group Hindu shopkeepers was due to internal reasons (e.g., they were honest men) while negative actions were the result of external reasons (e.g., cheating is a necessary business practice). However, when the actions were performed by out-group Muslim shopkeepers, the clerks gave the opposite reasons. In the undesirable situations, the Hindu clerks said that the reason was internal (the Muslims' poor characters)

and for the desirable ones, it was external (the situation). The researchers concluded from these findings that the Hindu clerks were able to maintain a positive image about their in-group by imagining especially good characteristics about their (Hindu) in-group and imagining negative characteristics about their (Muslim) out-group (Smith and Bond, 1994).

11 It is easy to imagine how the fundamental attribution error can cause misunderstandings. Let's say that you are talking to a man whom you don't know very well, and during your conversation, he does not make eye contact with you. You might think that he is shy or dishonest. However, the truth might be that in his culture, it is disrespectful to look directly at someone. In fact, he may have been showing you respect!

12 There is a tendency to view out-group members as being more homogeneous than the in-group members because we have less contact with out-group members. In other words, people tend to believe that members of an out-group all have a similar characteristic or personality. If a member of that out-group does something bad, we are apt to say it was because all of the members of that group have bad personalities. At the same time, we tend to see our in-group members as similar to us but with diverse characteristics. If a member of our in-group does something bad, we are likely to say that that individual was bad, but the rest of our group is still good.

13 We can see these varying attitudes regarding in-groups and out-groups in an incident that happened in Seattle, Washington. According to a news article, an electronics shop there falsely advertised that it would give free pick-up and delivery services for its customers, but in fact, it regularly charged them. On top of that, it misrepresented used equipment as new. It also charged customers for parts that were not needed or were not even installed. An American woman read this article and saw the owner's name. She said that she was not surprised because the owner was a member of an ethnic group and that this ethnic group cannot be trusted. When she found out that the owner of the shop was born in America, and in fact, his ancestors had come to America 180 years ago, she said that instead the owner was just a bad individual. (This was a personal experience by the authors of this book.)

Part 1: Study guide for Unit 12

1. In ¶ 1, the German student, Dieter, always put the money on the counter. What did the American student attribute this to?
   a) He thought Dieter did not like Blacks and did not want to touch their hands.
   b) He thought that in German culture, this is how people give money to a cashier.

2. What is the reason why Dieter put the money on the counter?
   a) He did not like Blacks and didn't want to touch their hands.
   b) In German culture, this is how people give money to a cashier.

3. In ¶ 2-6, the authors discuss the fundamental attribution error. Choose the statements that are true.
   a) If I make a mistake, I tend to think that I made it because of a negative aspect of my character.
   b) If I make a mistake, I tend to think that I made it because of a negative situation outside of me.
   c) If a stranger makes a mistake, I tend to think that he or she made it because of a negative aspect of that person's character.
   d) If a stranger makes a mistake, I tend to think that he or she made it because of a negative situation outside of that person.

For Questions 4 to 7, read the scenarios and circle the letters of the ones that explain the fundamental error of attribution.

4. Imagine that a man bought a used car. The next day, he realized that it was a bad car because it would not start. I would probably attribute this problem to ___ .
   a) this man's foolishness or laziness. He should have done more research before buying that car
   b) the dishonest salesman, who probably hid some problems with the car

5. I bought a used car. The next day, I realized that it was a bad car because it would not start. I would probably attribute this problem to ___ .
   a) my foolishness or laziness. I should have done more research before buying the car
   b) the dishonest salesman, who probably hid some problems with the car

6. I am a Mexican student, and I am studying in America. One day, I was walking on a path in a park; a group of three Americans were walking toward me. As they passed by me, I had to move off the path because the three Americans continued to walk next to each other. I would probably attribute this to the fact that ___.
   a) in general, Americans have bad manners
   b) the Americans were so deep in conversation that they did not see me

7. I am a Mexican student, and I am studying in America. One day, I was walking on a path in a park; a group of three Mexicans were walking toward me. As they passed by me, I had to move off the path because the three Mexicans continued to walk next to each other. I would probably attribute this to the fact that ___.
   a) in general, Mexicans have bad manners
   b) the Mexicans were so deep in conversation that they did not see me

8. This refers to ¶ 6. Let's say that I am very tall, and I ask you to give me a ride in your car. You say that you cannot. If I think that you said "no" because you have a prejudice against tall people, it means that I am attributing your action to ___.
   a) internal factors
   b) external factors

9. This item is about ¶ 8-10. Fill in the blanks with ***internal*** or ***external***.
   a) If we see a stranger do something good, for example pick up an empty can on the street, we are likely to think that he did it for ____________________ reasons.
   b) If we see a friend do something good, for example pick up an empty can on the street, we are likely to think that he did it for ____________________ reasons.

   c) If we see a stranger do something bad, for example get angry at a waiter, we are likely to think that he did it for ____________________ reasons.
   d) If we see a friend do something bad, for example get angry at a waiter, we are likely to think that he did it for ____________________ reasons.

10. This question is about ¶ 12-13. Imagine that a Canadian woman sees a man who is walking his dog, and he lets the dog make a mess in her yard. What will she think? (Choose all that apply.)
    a) If the man is a Korean, the Canadian woman is likely to think that, in general, Korean people do not know how to train a dog.
    b) If the man is a Canadian, the Canadian woman is likely to think that, in general, Canadian people do not know how to train a dog.
    c) If the man is a Korean, the Canadian woman is likely to think that that specific man does not know how to train his dog.
    d) If the man is a Canadian, the Canadian woman is likely to think that that specific man does not know how to train his dog.

11. Write one clarification question about a word, sentence, or idea that you do not understand in this unit. (If you understand everything, pretend that you don't.)

Part 2: Academic Vocabulary for Unit 12

Exercise 1

Words from context: Look at the paragraphs listed in the middle column of the chart below to find the words that have the meanings in the column on the right.

	Word	¶ *	Find the word that means . . .
1.		6	showing a special characteristic, emotion, or ability
2.		6	opposite
3.		12	varied; different from each other
4.		13	put a piece of equipment somewhere and make it ready to use
5.	(two words)	13	a group of people who share a common culture. They often share the same language, customs, and religion.

* **The symbol "¶" means paragraph.** You can find the word in that paragraph.

Exercise 2

Vocabulary Fill-in Exercise: Choose the words in Exercise 1 above to fill in the blanks below.

1. Paying for a purchase with a credit card, rather than cash, is often easier for a customer, but for a store owner, the ________________ is easier.
2. The hot water heater in Tom's apartment broke down, so a repairman ________________ a new one.
3. Vancouver is a city with a ________________ population. The people who are living there are from all over the world
4. When Hana was five years old, she started ________________ signs of being a genius, so she attends a school for especially smart children.
5. There are many ________________ in my neighborhood, so I can find a lot of different kinds of restaurants, for example, Chinese, Indian, Pakistani, Mexican, and Thai.

Exercise 3

Applied Vocabulary

1. Which of these are characteristics of someone who is exhibiting immaturity? (Choose all that apply.)
   a) He wants everyone to do what he wants to do.
   b) He understands others' points of view.
   c) He blames others when he makes a mistake.
   d) He cries when he watches sad movies.

2. Does your country have many ethnic groups? Explain.

3. Do you think that men are better leaders of a country than women, or the reverse? ______________ Why?

4. Do your friends these days have diverse backgrounds, or are most of them similar to each other? ____________________ Explain.

5. What software would you recommend that people install in their computers? ____________________ Explain.

Part 3: Preparation for discussion for Unit 12

Think about your answers to these questions. You do not have to write your answers.

1. In your country, do people give cashiers money directly into their hands, as Americans do, or put it on the counter, as Germans do?

2. Think of something that you had a problem with or a mistake that you made. Explain why you had this problem or made the mistake. We will tell you if you made a situation or personality attribution.

3. In ¶ 6, it says, "He sees the negative action of an out-group as caused by internal factors (their personalities or other traits)." Give me an example of when you attributed a negative action by someone as connected to their personality or other traits.

4. Tell us about a time when you got a low grade and the reason why you got the low grade. We will tell you if you made an internal or external attribution.

5. Do you sometimes have negative opinions about people from a foreign country?

❖ For "Small-group Discussion" questions in the form of Students A, B, and C, see ***Supplementary Activities***, or download it free from www.ProLinguaAssociates.com.

❖ For "Whole-class Discussion" techniques and a suggested procedure, see the ***Supplementary Activities***, or download it free from www.prolinguaassociates.com.

❖ For "Applied Outside-class Interactions/Observations," see the ***Supplementary Activities***, or download it free from www.prolinguaassociates.com.

Part 4: A technique for writing

Use the sandwich technique.

In this unit, you will learn about a technique that you can use to write essays for academic courses. It is called the sandwich technique, and it has three basic parts:

1) You write a quote from a source.
2) You explain what the quote means.
3) You explain how the quote is connected to your thesis statement.

You will practice these parts in this unit, and in the next unit, you will write an essay using the sandwich technique.

Explaining a Quote

Exercise 1

Match the quotes with their explanations below.

Quotes

a) "Minds are like parachutes. They only function when they are open."
b) "If a million people say a foolish thing, it is still a foolish thing."
c) "The most important thing in life is to learn how to give out love and to let it come in."

Explanations

___ 1) Many people think that to be really happy in life, we just need to help others. However, it's also important to allow others to help us. By allowing others to help us, other people get to experience the joy of being helpful.

___ 2) If we want to develop, we need to be willing to hear the opinions and ideas of people with whom we may not agree. If our minds are closed to new viewpoints, we will never expand our knowledge.

___ 3) It's very easy to follow the crowd. Often we do something, or believe in something, without thinking deeply about it. One reason for this is because a number of people whom we know do it or believe in it. However, just because a lot of people accept something does not mean that it is correct.

Exercise 2

Low-level students may just repeat the information in a quote, but advanced-level students explain the deeper meaning of the quote.

1) Write ***Good*** next to the explanations that tell the deeper meaning of a quote.
2) Write ***Repeated*** next to the explanations that just repeat the basic information in the quote.

1. *Quote*: **"If one finger is sore, the whole hand will hurt."**
   a) __Good__ If there is one member of a group who is in a bad mood, that person can have a negative effect on all the members.
   b) __Repeated__ If someone hurts their finger, their hand will feel pain.

2. ***Quote:* "I can get up in the morning and look at myself in the mirror, and my family can look at me too, and that's all that matters."**
   a) ____________ The most important thing for the author is that he feels good about himself and that his family believes that he is an honest person. However, if other people don't like him for some reason, that doesn't affect his self-esteem.
   b) ____________ Every day, when the author wakes up, he looks in the mirror, and his family looks at him too. What is important is that he can look at himself in the mirror.

3. *Quote*: **"Even fear of death is nothing compared to not having lived genuinely and fully."**
   a) ____________ The author believes that death is worse than not living fully.
   b) ____________ The author believes that when we are old, we will feel terrible if we realize that we have wasted our lives. A wasted life is worse than no life at all.

4. *Quote*: **"Few things are more exhilarating than to be shot at and missed."**
   a) ____________ In other words, it's important to try something new and perhaps something that is very difficult for us. We might not always be successful. However, if we can succeed, even if it takes luck to do it, we will have a great feeling of self-confidence. We will feel special.
   b) ____________ In other words, if someone shoots a gun at you, but they miss, you will feel wonderful. Very few people experience this. Thus, such an experience is an exciting one.

Exercise 3

Choose three quotes below and explain what they mean.

- Education is not the filling of a bucket, but the lighting of a fire.
- I may not have gone where I intended to go, but I think I have ended up where I needed to be.
- Anger makes you smaller, while forgiveness forces you to grow beyond what you were.
- The most important work you and I will ever do will be within the walls of our own homes.
- No one can make you feel inferior without your permission.
- There is no such thing as bad weather, only bad clothes.
- Poverty is the parent of revolution and crime.

Exercise 4

1) Read the "Information from a source" in the box.
2) Under the box, read the quote and choose the best explanation.

> ***Information from a source***
>
> "The central difference between collectivists and individualists is in how they view themselves. A collectivist sees himself as part of a group; his goals and the group's goals are the same. The individualist views himself as autonomous, or independent, from other people. If an individualist doesn't like the goals of the group that he belongs to, he will leave that group and join a different one" (Kehe & Kehe, 2014, p. 23).

1. ***Quote***: According to *Cultural Differences*, **"The central difference between collectivists and individualists is in how they view themselves."**

   1) Write ***Good*** next to the explanation that tells the deeper meaning of the quote.
   2) Write ***Repeated*** next to the explanation that just repeats information.

   a) ____________ The author is saying that a collectivist sees himself as part of a group; his goals and the group's goals are the same. The individualist views himself as autonomous, or independent, from others.

   b) ____________ The author is saying that in order to understand collectivists and individualists, we need to know about how each person views his or her identity. A collectivist identifies with a group. He wants and values the same things that his group members want and value. On the other hand, an individualist decides by himself what he wants and what is important to him.

Exercise 5

1) Read the "Information from a source" in the box.
2) Under the box, read the quote and choose the best explanation.

> ***Information from a source***
>
> "While collectivists feel happiest when their in-group does well, an individualist feels most pleasure when he himself is successful. An individualist might say, 'What is best for me is important'"(Kehe & Kehe, 2014, p. 79).

Quote: Kehe & Kehe state, **"While collectivists feel happiest when their in-group does well, an individualist feels more pleasure when he himself is successful."**

1) Write ***Good*** next to the explanation that tells the deeper meaning of the quote.
2) Write ***Repeated*** next to the explanation that just repeats the ideas from the quote.

a) ____________ According to the author, if a group of collectivists is trying to accomplish something, and if they are successful, each member will feel pleasure. For example, let's say that five members are trying to raise $500 for their club. If they get $500, they will all feel satisfied, no matter how much each individual raised. However, an individualist would not feel satisfied unless he himself raised at least his share of the $500, in other words, at least $100.

b) ____________ According to the author, in a collectivist group, if the in-group does something good, the collectivist will feel pleasure. However, an individualist will feel happy if he does something very well by himself.

Exercise 6

Read the quote and write an explanation.

Quote: The author points out, **". . . compliments can cause problems in groups because they encourage comparisons."**

Exercise 7

1) Find a quote either in *Cultural Differences* or from a different source.
2) Introduce the quote by using an expression from the box below.
3) Explain what the author is saying.

Expressions for introducing a quote

- The author states, . . .
- Stevens mentions, . .
- The article says, ...
- According to the author, ...
- Thomas observes, ...
- According to the article, ...
- Johnson suggests, . . .
- The author points out, . . .
- Jones believes, ...
- Smith explained, ...
- The article reports, ...
- The author argues ...

Explain how a quote is connected to your thesis statement

Exercise 8

Read each thesis statement, quote, and explanation. Then choose the best paragraph that relates to the thesis statement.

1. *Thesis statement*: **Differences in cultural values can be an important reason for conflicts in international companies.**

Quote ⇨ **Explanation of the quote ⇨**	The article states, "The central difference between collectivists and individualists is in how they view themselves." The author is saying that in order to understand collectivists and individualists, we need to know about how each person views his or her identity. A collectivist identifies with a group. He wants and values the same things that his group members want and value. On the other hand, an individualist decides by himself what he wants and what is important to him. *(To the student: Here, the writer will connect the quote to the thesis statement above.)*

1) Write ***Good*** next to the good connection to the thesis statement.
2) Write ***Weak*** next to the poor connection to the thesis statement.

a) ________________ If we ask an individualist and a collectivist to work together in an international company, it is possible that there will be a conflict because of these differences. The collectivist will probably want to make decisions together with the individualist, but the individualist will prefer to make his own decisions.

b) ________________ I am a collectivist, so I prefer to work with my group members. For example, last weekend, I wanted to stay home and read a book, but my in-group members wanted to take a trip to Vancouver. Since that is what my group members wanted, I decided to join them.

2. *Thesis statement*: **Because of different cultural values, a business in an individualist country is more likely to be successful than one in a collectivist country.**

Quote ⇨ **Explaining the quote ⇨**	Kehe & Kehe points out, "While collectivists feel happiest when their in-group does well, an individualist feels more pleasure when he himself is successful." If a group of collectivists is trying to accomplish something, and if they are successful, each member will feel pleasure. For example, let's say that five members are trying to raise $500 for their club. If they get $500, they will all feel satisfied, no matter how much each individual raised. However, an individualist would not feel satisfied unless he himself raised at least his share of the $500, in other words, at least $100. *(To the student: Here, the writer will connect the quote to the thesis statement above.)*

1) Write ***Good*** next to the good connection to the thesis statement.
2) Write ***Weak*** next to the poor connection to the thesis statement.

a) ________________ In a collectivist country, the members will not be upset if a member does not accomplish as much as the others. They will see that each member has other positive characteristics. Nevertheless, an individualist might be upset at a "weaker" member. This person would also feel disappointed in himself if he was less successful than his group members.

b) ________________ If we apply these ideas to business, we can see that in a collectivist country, weak workers will continue to have a job as long as the company is successful. In a company in an individualist country, each individual will be expected to perform successfully. If someone does not, he will lose his job. For this reason, the business will keep the best workers and will probably be more successful.

Part 5: Preview for Unit 13

1. Imagine that a young man is living far away from his family and friends. One day, he murders someone. Which of these would you be apt to say is the reason why he did this?

    a) Because of his personality
    b) Because he didn't have support from his family and friends

2. Would you prefer to marry someone older or younger than you? ________________

3. Let's say that you are taking a course in college. You study very hard and often stay up late at night. You do all your assignments and come to class every day. However, you are not able to pass the tests. Let's also say that you have a classmate who is the reverse of you. He doesn't study much, sometimes skips class and doesn't do all his homework. He also fails the tests. What should happen to you and your classmate?

    a) I should be allowed to pass the course.
    b) My classmate and I should both fail the course.

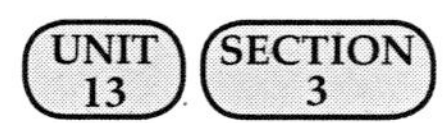

Unit 13

13.1 Groups

Group responsibility vs. individual responsibility

Reading

[1] Researchers presented this imaginary situation to some Asian and American subjects: A young man was living far away from home and did not have any close family members or friends near him. He was found guilty of murdering some people in the city where he lived. They then asked the subjects to imagine what conditions led to these murders and how the murders could have been prevented. Compared to the Americans, the Asians were much more likely to say that the young man's isolated social situation was an important factor. In other words, they felt that the young man might not have committed that terrible crime if he had had stronger in-group support. For example, the Asians were more likely to choose these:

The young man would not have committed the murder _____

✓ if he had stayed at his former work organization
✓ if he had belonged to a religious group
✓ if he had friends and relatives who lived nearby
✓ if he had been married with children

[2] On the other hand, the Americans were more apt to say that the young man committed the murders because of his personality and that he would have committed the terrible act even if his social situation had not been so isolated (Morris and Peng, 1994).

13.2 Relationships

Horizontal vs. vertical

[3] People who believe that the most important relationship in their life is between a husband and wife, or between a parent and child, often assume everyone in the world would agree with them. However, this is not necessarily true. In order to explore the concept of relationships, answer the questions in the questionnaire below.

Questionnaire

1. How would you rank the most important relationships in your culture? (Put a "1" next to the most important relationship, a "2" next to the second most important, and a "3" next to the third.)

   ___ mother and child
   ___ father and child
   ___ husband and wife
   ___ other: ____________________

2. Imagine that you are studying in the U.S. You are having some difficulties with your landlord and are having problems solving them. Who would you feel more comfortable asking for help with your problem? (Choose one answer below.)

   ___ an instructor or advisor
   ___ an American friend

4 According to cross-cultural studies, the relationship between the parent and child is considered closer in collectivist cultures, whereas the relationship between a husband and wife is considered closer in individualist ones. Triandis (1994b) illustrates this difference by citing this example. A 21-year-old Vietnamese, whose father was an American soldier and mother was Vietnamese, decided to emigrate to the U.S. Although he was given permission by the U.S. government to move to the U.S., he was told that he could bring only one relative, his mother or his wife. Since Vietnam is a collectivist country, in which the parent-child relationship is closer than the husband-wife relationship, it's not surprising that even though he was married, he chose to bring his mother. This story had a happy ending for everyone. Because the U.S. is an individualist country, in which the husband-wife relationship is highly valued, the U.S. government decided to let him also bring his wife. Interestingly, if his first choice had been to bring his wife, he probably would have had a more difficult time convincing the U.S. government to allow him to also bring his mother.

5 The most-valued relationship can, in fact, vary widely from culture to culture. In China, the father-son is most important. In India, Mexico and Greece, it's the mother-son. In some parts of Africa, the relationship between an older and younger brother is the most. There is even a culture where the most important relationship is between a mother-in-law and son-in-law; that culture is in northern Australia, in a tribe called the Tiwi (Triandis, 1994b).

6 Collectivists, in general, tend to view the parent-child relationship as having the highest priority, while individualists are more apt to consider the spouse-spouse (i.e., husband-wife) relationship to have the highest value. Because of this difference, a marriage between a collectivist and individualist can be difficult, especially between a collectivist male and individualist female. As we saw in the example above about the Vietnamese man who chose to take his mother (rather than his wife) with him to America, the collectivist husband will view the mother-son relationship as most important, whereas the individualist wife will feel that the relationship between her husband and herself, rather than between her husband and his mother, should be the top priority. This type of marriage has a greater chance of being successful if the mother-in-law lives far away from the couple, for example, in a different country or if she is no longer living. However, if she is living near them, there is an increased possibility that the marriage will end in a divorce, when compared to other types of marriages. In fact, the type of marriage least likely to end in divorce is one between two collectivists. The next strongest marriages are between two individualists, and the one most likely to fail is between an individualist wife and collectivist husband (Triandis, 1988)

7 Another way to look at these differing relationships is: The most important relationships in collectivist cultures are vertical, for example, between a parent and child, in which one is considered in a higher, or superior, role and the other is in a lower, or subordinate, position. In individualist cultures, the most important relationships are horizontal, for example between two spouses, or between two friends. In other words, the husband and wife, or two friends, are considered to be equal.

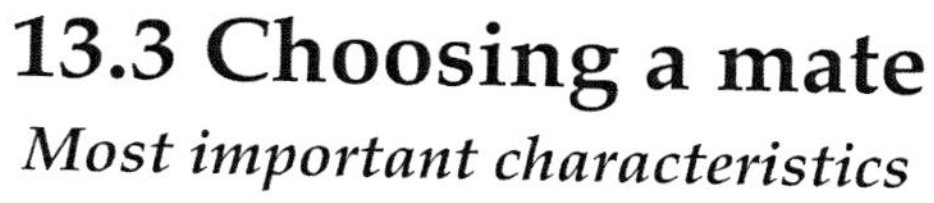

13.3 Choosing a mate

Most important characteristics

8 If you were looking for a future spouse, what would be the most important characteristics that you would want in a husband or wife? Answer these questions:

1. Whom would you prefer to be older: yourself or your spouse? ________________
2. How many years older, or younger, would you prefer your spouse to be?
   ______ years older/young.
3. Evaluate the following factors in choosing a future spouse. Write a number in each blank. (If you prefer not to rate them, put an "X" in the blanks.)

◆ necessary:	3 points
◆ important but not necessary:	2 points
◆ wanted but not very important:	1 point
◆ not important:	0 points

____ physically attractive
____ kind and understanding
____ exciting personality
____ intelligent
____ good ability to earn money
____ chastity (i.e., no previous sexual experience)
____ healthy
____ religious
____ good at keeping the house clean
____ wants children
____ good family background
____ college graduate
____ easy-going
____ creative and artistic

9 Researchers interviewed people in 37 countries about important characteristics in a future spouse and found that nearly everywhere respondents agreed about the most important characteristics: kind and understanding, intelligent, exciting personality, and healthy.

10 The biggest difference in how countries rated the importance of an item was regarding chastity (i.e., no previous sexual experience). Men and women from the Netherlands and Scandinavian countries (e.g., Sweden and Norway) said it was not important. In fact, some people wrote that it was not desirable to marry someone who had had no previous experience with sexual intercourse! On the other hand, in China, India, Taiwan and Iran, respondents said chastity was very important. People in Japan, Poland and Colombia saw chastity as moderately desirable (wanted but not very important). Interestingly, in all countries, men tend to value chastity in their partners more than women do.

[11] Cultures around the world shared these general preferences. Women put a priority on choosing a spouse who had the ability to earn money. Men all over the world tended to put more value on a partner's physical attractiveness than women did.

[12] Men preferred spouses who were younger than them, and fortunately, women preferred husbands who were older. The reason for this might be because men become mature at a later age than women, and women are likely to prefer a mature mate; also, women might find older men more appealing as, thanks to their greater wealth, they can provide more opportunities for the couple's children (Buss, 1994).

Part 1: Study guide for Unit 13

1. This refers to ¶ 1 and 2. Imagine that a man had to enter a hospital because of stress. I asked some of his neighbors, individualists and collectivists, why they think he felt so much stress. Who do you think gave the reasons below?

   In the blanks next to the reasons, write ***collectivists*** or ***individualists***.

   a) He was kind of strange. ________________

   b) He didn't have a wife. ________________

   c) His parents lived 10 hours away from him. ________________

   d) He thought that he was smarter than other people, so he often had arguments.

   ____

   e) He moved to that neighborhood recently and didn't have any friends.

   ____

2. In ¶ 4, the story about the Vietnamese who emigrated to the U.S. demonstrates that ___.
   a) a husband-wife relationship is the most important for Vietnamese
   b) a parent-child relationship is the most important for Vietnamese
   c) all relationships are equally important for Vietnamese and Americans

3. According to ¶ 6, which type of marriages have the best chance of success. (Write a number "1" next to best chance, a number "2" next to the second best chance, etc.)

   ___• an individualist man and an individualist woman
   ___• a collectivist man and an individualist woman
   ___• a collectivist man and a collectivist woman

4. Describe these relationships. Fill in the blanks with ***horizontal*** or ***vertical***.
   a) Lee and his girlfriend, Anna: ________________ relationship
   b) Lee and his boss: ________________ relationship
   c) Lee and his math instructor: ________________ relationship
   d) Lee and his twin brother: ________________ relationship
   e) Lee and his best friend, Juan: ________________ relationship
   f) Lee and his father: ________________ relationship

5. According to ¶ 9, concerning characteristics of a future spouse, what did people in most countries agree on? The spouse should ___. (Choose all that apply.)

   a) be intelligent
   b) earn enough money
   c) be healthy
   d) be an exciting person
   e) have no previous sexual experience

6. Who valued chastity more? (Choose one answer in each item.)

   a) ___ Chinese (or) ___ Japanese
   b) ___ Swedes (or) ___ Colombians
   c) ___ men (or) ___ women

7. This is about ¶ 11-12. Fill in the blanks with ***men*** or ***women***.

   ____________________ a) Who thought beauty was more important?

   ____________________ b) Who wanted a younger spouse?

   ____________________ c) Who wanted a spouse who could earn a lot of money?

   ____________________ d) Who wanted an older spouse?

8. Write one clarification question about a word, sentence, or idea that you do not understand in this unit. (If you understand everything, pretend that you don't.)

Part 2: Academic Vocabulary for Unit 13

Exercise 1

Words from context: Look at the paragraphs listed in the middle column of the chart below to find the words that have the meanings in the column on the right.

	Word	¶ *	Find the word that means . . .
1.		1	did (such as "a crime")
2.		4	making someone agree with an idea
3.		6	husband or wife
4.		6	the important need, plan, or element
5.		7	at the same level

* **¶ means paragraph number.** You can find the word in that paragraph.

Exercise 2

Vocabulary Fill-in Exercise: Choose the words in Exercise 1 above to fill in the blanks below.

1. Sam's top ____________________ for exercising is to build big muscles.
2. Tina, Alex, and Cindy started a band, but none of them is the leader. They all feel equal. They have a ____________________ relationship.
3. My office had a party, and everyone who was married brought their ____________.
4. Many people think that a person who ____________________ murder should receive the death penalty.
5. It is sometimes hard to ____________________ elderly people to stop driving because, often, they don't realize that their skills have declined.

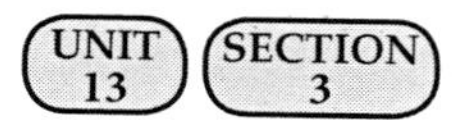

Exercise 3

Applied Vocabulary

1. Among your group of close friends, is your relationship horizontal, or is one of you a leader of your group? Explain.

2. Was it difficult for you to convince your parents to let you study at this school? ____ What did you do to convince them that it was a good idea?

3. Tell about someone who committed a crime.

4. What is your highest priority for studying at this school?

5. If you get married, would you like your spouse to be active and enjoy being around people a lot (i.e., an extrovert), or prefer to have quiet time and often like to be alone with you (i.e., an introvert)? Explain.

Part 3: Preparation for discussion for Unit 13

Think about your answers to these questions. You do not have to write your answers.

1. In ¶ 1, there is a discussion about a murder. Do you agree with the Chinese or American reason for the murder? Explain.

2. Imagine that you are a man. If you had to choose whether to bring your mother or wife to the U.S., which would you choose?

3. In ¶ 5, it discusses the most valuable relationships in different cultures. Were any of these surprising to you?

4. What is the most important relationship for you?

5. If you married someone from a different culture, do you think that there would be problems between your spouse and your mother? Explain.

6. Would you like to marry someone from a different culture? Explain.

7. If you are a collectivist, would you like to marry an individualist or vice versa?

8. Look at the questionnaire in ¶ 8. Be prepared to explain your reasons.

9. Were you surprised by the results concerning chastity in ¶ 10? Explain.

❖ For "Small-group Discussion" questions in the form of Students A, B, and C, see *Supplementary Activities*, or download it free from www.ProLinguaAssociates.com.

❖ For "Whole-class Discussion" techniques and a suggested procedure, see the *Supplementary Activities*, or download it free from www.prolinguaassociates.com.

❖ For "Applied Outside-class Interactions/Observations," see the *Supplementary Activities*, or download it free from www.prolinguaassociates.com.

Part 4: A technique for writing

Apply the sandwich technique.

In Unit 12, you studied the sandwich technique for academic papers. In this unit, you will look at two outlines, analyze a model paper using this technique, and then write an essay using it.

Topic: If you were a boss of an international company, would you prefer to hire workers who are collectivists or individualists?

Exercise 1

Look at the two thesis statements and outlines below. After writing the outlines, the writer will choose to write an essay about one of them.

Thesis statement: I would prefer to hire collectivist workers.

- ◆ Collectivists are more loyal to their group (Unit 2.2).
- ◆ They try to develop harmony (2.2) and will conform to maintain it (4).
- ◆ They usually are from tight cultures, so they will follow rules (5.1).
- ◆ If there is a conflict, they tend to choose compromise over confrontation (9.2).
- ◆ They feel that success comes from hard work rather than ability (11.1).

Thesis statement: I would prefer to hire individualist workers.

- ◆ Individualists are able to work independently (Unit 2.2).
- ◆ They use compliments more (6.2).
- ◆ They are not so "tight," so they might be tolerant of others (5.1).
- ◆ They recognize individual excellence in others (5.2).
- ◆ They value honesty over harmony (8.2).

Exercise 2

The writer chose one of the topics above and wrote the essay under the box. Read the essay and fill in the blanks with the words in the box.

Paragraphs 1-2	
◆ The authors are saying that individualists	◆ would prefer to hire individualist workers
◆ As a boss, I would	◆ According to *Cultural*
Paragraph 3	
◆ Kehe & Kehe (2014) state,	◆ technique for my workers
◆ He appreciated my compliment,	◆ communication" (p. 37). In other
Paragraphs 4-5	
◆ these goals most effectively	◆ improvement" (Kehe & Kehe, 2014, p. 102).
◆ to be successful, I believe that	◆ I would want employees who

Hiring Workers	Parts of the essay
[1] In this time of globalization, international companies are looking all over the world for the best workers. Those workers will not only have high skills but also will be successful at interacting with people who are from other countries. Therefore, if I were the boss of such a company, I ______________________________ ______________.	*Thesis statement*
[2] A good worker should have confidence to make decisions by himself. ______________ ______ *Differences*, "The individualist views himself as autonomous, or independent, from other people" (p.15). ______________________ do not need other people to tell them what to think or do. They believe in themselves and feel that they have the ability to make smart decisions on their own. ____ ______________want a worker like this. Let's say that it is 5:00 p.m. on a Friday. The phone rings. It is a customer who is calling from overseas. He is having problems with an expensive tool that our company has sold him, and he needs a replacement immediately. If we wait five minutes, it will be too late to ship it to that customer until Monday. I myself have already left the office. I would expect one of my workers to quickly make the decision about whether or not to send the replacement tool without having to discuss it with anyone else.	______________ ______________ *Explanation of 1st quote* *Relating 1st quote to thesis statement*
[3] Another important characteristic of a good employee is the ability to develop relationships with customers. ______________ "Individualists often change groups. In order to join a new group, they might use compliments to charm outsiders and open new avenues of ______________	______________ ______________

____________words, individualists try to develop the technique of complimenting, which they can use to establish relationships with other people. For example, they might praise someone for something that that person did or even for what that person is wearing. This can make the other person feel good. This would be a useful ________________________________ to know. If they can make a positive comment or observation about a customer, that customer will probably have a good impression of our company in general. For instance, I used to work in a shoe store. One day, I was talking to a customer, and I mentioned that I liked his gold watch, which looked very stylish. ________________________ ________________________________ and I believe that he thought I had good taste. As a result, I think that he trusted my opinion about which shoes he should buy.	______________________ *Relating 2nd quote to thesis statement*
4) Finally, ______________________________________ will tell me if they see any problems in the company. In a study, observers watched international and Americans students who were doing peer-editing with classmates. The observers found, "…the Americans were direct in their remarks. They pointed out specific weaknesses in the essay and made suggestions for _____________ ________________________________ This means that the Americans told their opinions as clearly as they could. They felt that their classmates would benefit from their comments even if they were criticisms. For a company __________________________________ ______________________it's necessary to have workers with this kind of attitude. I don't want workers who will make only observations and comments that will make me happy, especially if there are problems that I need to	*Third topic sentence* ______________________ ______________________ ______________________

know about. One of the best ways to improve a company is to fix anything that decreases our productivity, and the first step is for us to know what we need to fix. 5) In conclusion, collectivists and individualists have strong points and weak points. Anyone who is a boss needs to know what kind of employee will help the company make a good product, keep customers happy, and improve the performance of the company in general. If I were a boss, I could accomplish ________________ ________________________________with individualist workers. ***Reference*** Kehe, D., & Kehe, P. (2014). *Cutural Differences.* Brattleboro, Vt.: Pro Lingua.	______________________

Exercise 3

Look at Exercise 1 again. In the right column is "Parts of the Essay." Fill in the blanks with the words in the box below:

✓◆ Thesis statement ◆ 1st quote ◆ 2nd quote ◆ 3rd quote
◆ 1st topic sentence ◆ 2nd topic sentence ✓◆ 3rd topic sentence
✓◆ Explanation of 1st quote ◆ Explanation of 2nd quote
◆ Explanation of 3rd quote ✓◆ Relating 1st quote to thesis statement
✓◆ Relating 2nd quote to thesis statement ◆ Relating 3rd quote to thesis statement
◆Conclusion

Exercise 4

Write an essay and use the sandwich technique. Use information from this textbook, *Cultural Differences*, to support your ideas.

Step 1: Choose one of the topics in the box below for your essay.

- Which is a better country to live in: a collectivist or individualist country?
- In which country do people feel more stress: a collectivist or an individualist country?
- Which is a better country for children to grow up in: a collectivist or an individualist country?
- If someone from ____________________ *(name of a country)* was planning to live for a few years in ____________________ *(name of a country)*, that person should understand some cross-cultural aspects in order to have a successful experience.

Step 2: Use this organization for your essay.

1) Write an introduction and thesis statement.
2) Write 2-5 paragraphs of support for your thesis. In each of the paragraphs, you should:
   1 start with a topic sentence.
   2 quote from *Cultural Differences*.
   3 explain what the authors mean by that quote.
   4 relate the quote to your thesis statement.
3) Write a conclusion.
4) Include "Source Cited" at the end of your paper:
   Kehe, D., & Kehe, P. (2014). *Cultural Differences*. Brattleboro, Vt.: Pro Lingua.

(Look at the sample essay, "Hiring Workers," on p. 193-195 for a model of how you can write this essay.)

Part 5: Preview for Unit 14

1. Imagine that you are walking on a quiet sidewalk in your country, and you see a stranger walking toward you. Will you smile at the stranger? (Choose one.)
   a) often b) sometimes c) rarely d) never

2. Which of these would make you the happiest?
   a) I have close friends whom I can depend on.
   b) I work hard at something, and I achieve my dream.

3. What makes a good relationship?
   a) Harmony. In other words, a person considers what other people need and want.
   b) Each person in a relationship remains independent while trying to get along with each other. "Being yourself" in a relationship is necessary.

4. Read the situations below and rate your feelings about them on a 7-point scale:
   1 = I don't agree with the statement ⇨ 7 = I strongly agree with the statement.

   ___ Children should always take pride in their personal achievement.
   ___ Children should be encouraged to take pride only in achievement that benefits others.
   ___ A child who expresses pride in personal accomplishments will not be respected by peers.

Unit 14

14.1 Showing emotions

smile and frown

Reading

[1] A college student in America was looking at pictures of her Russian parents when they were still living in Russia during the 1970s. Many of the pictures were taken during happy times at weddings, parties and vacations. However, she noticed something surprising. Nobody was smiling. When she asked her mother the reason why, she replied, "We don't smile in pictures" (Koren, 2010).

[2] According to research, Russians, followed by Japanese and South Koreans, control their facial emotions more than people from other countries, and Americans control theirs the least (Matsumoto, 2006). In addition, facial expressions are acceptable or unacceptable depending on the place. In America, it's normal to smile at a stranger, but if someone frowns at a stranger, it is considered rude. On the other hand, in Russia, frowning at a stranger is considered normal, but smiling is considered suspicious.

[3] Studies show that in countries like Russia, Japan, and South Korea, where strong control of facial expressions is the norm, people focus on each other's eyes when they interpret someone else's emotions. On the other hand, in countries like the United States,

where emotions are more freely expressed, people focus on the other person's mouth. Interestingly, when people from these countries try to express emotions in emails or text messages, they use "emoticons" that depict the eyes or mouth. Japanese will use these emoticons, which focus on the eyes: happy face (^_^) or sad face (;_;), but Americans typically use these emoticons, which focus on the mouth: happy face :) or sad face :((Science Daily, 2007).

4 Individualists and collectivists tend to interpret smiles differently. Researchers showed pictures to American and Asian subjects of whites and Asians who were either smiling or were neutral. The subjects were asked to rate whether the people in the pictures looked attractive, sociable, or intelligent. The Americans said that the people who were smiling looked more attractive, sociable, and intelligent, compared to those with neutral faces. Similarly, the Asians rated the ones with smiles as more attractive and sociable. However, they said that the ones with a neutral expression looked more intelligent (Shiraev and Levy, 2001).

14.2 Feeling emotions

Pride and shame

5 This is a questionnaire concerning your feelings about pride and shame.

Questionnaire

Directions

Read the situations below and rate your feelings about them on a 7-point scale:

1 = I don't agree with the statement. ⇨ 7 = I strongly agree with the statement.

___ Situation 1: I would feel proud if I were accepted to a prestigious university.

___ Situation 2: I would feel proud if my child were accepted at a prestigious university.

___ Situation 3: In a sports event, I would feel proud if I performed well, but my team lost.

___ Situation 4: In a sports event, I would feel proud if I performed poorly, but my team won.

___ Situation 5: If I were caught cheating on a test, I would feel shame.

___ Situation 6: If my brother were caught cheating on a test, I would feel shame.

6 Stipek (1998) reported on a study in which researchers gave the hypothetical situations that are listed above to 200 college students in China and the United States. The Chinese experienced more pride when others were successful while the American students tended to feel more pride in personal accomplishments.

7 In Situations 1 and 2 (about acceptance to a prestigious university), the Americans rated them as equal, but the Chinese felt more pride if their child were accepted.

8 In Situations 3 and 4 (about the sports event), the Americans felt more pride when they performed well, but the Chinese said they felt more pride when their team won.

9 In Situations 5 and 6 (about cheating), the Chinese felt greater shame in both situations than the Americans felt.

10 Researchers also gave American and Chinese students some statements concerning pride that children should feel and express. The statements are the ones that you responded to in the Preview for Unit 14, Question 4 on p.197. These are the results:

Rate on a 7-point scale your degree of agreement.

1 = I don't agree with the statement. ⇨ 7 = I strongly agree with the statement.

Statement	Chinese (n=101) Average score	Americans (n=78) Average score
Children should always take pride in their personal achievement.	3.7	6.1
Children should be encouraged to take pride only in achievement that benefits others·	5.6	2.9
A child who expresses pride in personal accomplishments will not be respected by peers·	5.7	2.5

11 In sum, it appears that Americans view personal accomplishments as sources of pride, whereas Chinese experience more pride in others' accomplishments than Americans do.

14.3 Happiness

Different causes

12 What would you say "happiness" is? Choose one:

____ a) "Happiness" is getting along with other people, being accepted by society, being cared for, and not being isolated.

____ b) "Happiness" is doing what I want to do and not being limited by society; it is being rewarded for all the hard work that I do.

13 Researchers conducted studies in which they asked Chinese and American students to write an essay. The assigned topic was: Explain what happiness is. The Chinese students' descriptions tended to be similar to Item "a" (above) while the Americans' descriptions had more in common with Item "b" (Lu and Gilmour, 2004).

14 According to recent studies (Shu and Oishi, 2002; Lu and Gilmour, 2004; Uchida et al, 2004), cultures have different definitions of what happiness means and how a person can achieve it. In general, collectivists tend to feel that social integration leads to greater happiness, whereas, individualists believe that happiness comes from the freedom to choose what they themselves want to do.

15 In the studies cited in paragraph 14, both Americans and Chinese felt that the individual is responsible for their own happiness. However, there were some differences. Americans felt that happiness comes from the ability to control their destiny. In other words, Americans believe that they can gain happiness if they are able to influence the people around them and affect the events in their own lives. It comes from self-autonomy, in which one has a great amount of freedom to fulfill what one wants to achieve. At the foundation of this attitude is the belief that a person can actively pursue happiness and that happiness is a reward for personal hard work. The actor Brad Pitt is an example of this. He was studying journalism in college but decided to pursue acting instead. He had only one more semester before graduating, and his college instructors were urging him to stay in school and get his degree. However, he ignored their advice, quit school, and moved 1,000 miles away to pursue his dream in Hollywood. Today, he is one of the most famous actors in the U.S. (Bartimus, 2002).

16 On the other hand, for Asians, complete freedom does not exist. A person, they believe, has to accept whatever life brings. In fact, many Chinese students feel that happiness comes from being open to—and grateful for—their fate (Lu and Gilmour, 2004).

17 For collectivists, perhaps the most important source of happiness is social relationships. These relationships are not confined to just their immediate family and close friends but also to others around them. For collectivists, two people can unite with

each other and realize their inter-dependence, i.e., realize how they can depend on each other for mutual gain. Researchers studied the happiness levels of a variety of groups in Calcutta, India, including students who were from middle-class families and people who were very poor slum-dwellers. Not surprisingly, the slum-dwellers were not satisfied with their food or living conditions. However, their level of happiness was similar to the level of the middle-class students! The researchers think that the reason for the high level of happiness among the slum-dwellers could be attributed to the strong social support that their extended families provide (Biswas-Diener and Diener, 2001).

Family life on a Calcutta street

18 Asians feel that happiness comes from harmony, and harmony comes when people restrain from pursuing their own goals and desires and, instead, consider what other people need and want. Collectivists will consider a personal form of happiness to be incomplete, so they do not place as much importance on it. For them, complete happiness comes from a relationship with others in which there is harmony and support. Instead of someone deciding for oneself what will lead to happiness, it is more often decided by the in-group

19 Suh and Oishi (2002) cite an example from Korea in order to illustrate how the collectivist society there shapes the viewpoint of young people regarding what is necessary to feel happiness. Many Korean teenagers believe there is only one thing that will make them and other people in their lives truly happy and that is to be admitted to a top university. This is unlike the attitude in individualist societies, where each person feels a greater sense of freedom to decide what happiness means.

20 Interestingly, in the study cited above in ¶ 12-13, involving the assigned essay topic on happiness, in the Americans' essays, they never used an expression like "harmony" when describing happiness. For Americans, in a good relationship, each person maintains independence while still trying to get along with others. Americans feel that "being yourself" is vital for a healthy relationship.

21 According to Asians, happiness and unhappiness are closely related. They depend on each of the two emotions. By contrasting the two emotions, they get deeper meaning about life experiences. The meanings of the two are continually changing, from an Asian point of view. On the other hand, individualists perceive any kind of negative feelings or personal failings as an obstacle to happiness. They will be surprised to learn that collectivists can interpret a personal failure as a positive event, because even a negative experience like a personal failure can open a path to happiness. And collectivists believe that this path can lead to an opportunity to receive support from others and to show compassion to others. In contrast, individualists will see the need for support from others as a weakness. Individualists will make great efforts to minimize unpleasant emotions, whereas collectivists have a greater ability to accept a balance between positive and negative situations. In general, Asians do not believe that feeling happy is as important as individualists do. They tend to worry less often about whether they are happy or satisfied with life. In fact, unlike Americans, feeling "ordinary" is a happy emotion for collectivists (Lu and Gilmour, 2004).

Part 1: Study guide for Unit 14

1. In ¶ 2, there is a discussion about smiling and frowning. Fill in the chart with "normal" or "strange."

	Smile at a stranger	Frown at a stranger
Russians		
Americans		

2. According to ¶ 3, the "emoticons" that people use show that ___. (Choose all that apply.)
   a) Asians focus on people's eyes to discover what emotions they are feeling
   b) Asians focus on people's mouths to discover what emotions they are feeling
   c) Americans focus on people's eyes to discover what emotions they are feeling
   d) Americans focus on people's mouths to discover what emotions they are feeling

3. In ¶ 6-14, the authors discuss pride and happiness. Fill in the blanks with "A Chinese" or "An American."

   a. ____________________ is likely to say, "I feel most proud when I do something well."

   b. ____________________ is likely to say, "I feel most proud when others in my in-group do something well."

   c. ____________________ is likely to say, "I recently received scholarship offers from two colleges. At one college, I will get the scholarship if I play basketball. At the other one, I need to major in math to get it. My parents advised me to take the basketball one, but I decided to take the one in math. I'm very happy about my decision."

   d. ____________________ is likely to say, "I recently received scholarship offers from two colleges. At one college, I will get the scholarship if I play basketball. At the other one, I need to major in math to get it. I enjoy basketball and am confident that I can do well, but my parents advised me to take the one in math. I don't feel very confident about that subject, but I have some friends at that college who invited me to join a study group. I decided to take the math scholarship, and I'm happy about my decision."

4. According to ¶ 17, the slum-dwellers had high levels of happiness because ___.
   a) they had enough food to eat, and their houses were comfortable
   b) they had the freedom to move to a different place if they preferred
   c) they knew that if they worked hard, their situation would improve
   d) they had family members who helped them when they needed it

5. According to ¶ 18-19, ___.
   a) individualists do not like other people
   b) individualists feel that, in a healthy relationship, each person should feel free to have their own ideas
   c) individualists are happiest when their in-group members are successful

6. Collectivists are most likely to feel happy when ___.
   a) they are doing what society has decided will bring happiness
   b) they are free to make their own decisions
   c) they feel personally successful in what they are trying to accomplish

7. According to ¶ 21, if individualists have a bad experience, ___.
   a) they tend to feel that it is robbing them of happiness
   b) they tend to see it as a chance to learn something that will lead them to happiness in the future

8. According to ¶ 21, if collectivists have a bad experience, ___.
   a) they tend to feel that it is robbing them of happiness
   b) they tend to see it as a chance to learn something that will lead them to happiness in the future

9. Write one clarification question about a word, sentence, or idea that you do not understand in this unit. (If you understand everything, pretend that you don't.)

Part 2: Academic Vocabulary for Unit 14

Exercise 1

Words from context: Look at the paragraphs listed in the middle column of the chart below to find the words that have the meanings in the column on the right.

	Word	¶ *	Find the word that means . . .
1.		4	lacking in emotion; unemotional
2.		11	a place or thing that something comes from
3.		15	base; basic idea or principle
4.	(two words)	17	a benefit that two or more people can enjoy
5.		18	stop someone from doing something (usually in a physical sense)

* **The symbol "¶" means paragraph.** You can find the word in that paragraph.

Exercise 2

Vocabulary Fill-in Exercise: Choose the words in Exercise 1 above to fill in the blanks below.

1. Sue is good at planning, and Sara finds it easy to talk to strangers, so there is a ________________ when they travel together.

2. When Tina told her husband, Dan, that she was going to have a baby, his reaction was ________________, so she didn't think that he heard what she had said.

3. The ________________ of good health is to make smart life-style choices.

4. If you are trying to teach a dog good manners, it's important to ________________ it from jumping up on people.

5. Fruits are a good ________________ of vitamins.

Exercise 3

Applied Vocabulary

1. What do you think is the foundation of a good marriage?

2. Choose at least one of these and answer it:
   a) What is a good source if you are looking for music to listen to?
   b) What is a good source for news?
   c) What is a useful source for information if you are planning a vacation?

3. If your family members hear happy or surprising news, do they all show a lot of emotion, or do some of them tend to look neutral?

4. Think of a person whom you know. What is his/her name? ________________
   Does your relationship have mutual gain, or does one of you benefit more from the relationship? Explain.

5. What junk food is (or was) difficult for you to restrain yourself from eating?

❖ For "Small-group Discussion" questions in the form of Students A, B, and C, see ***Supplementary Activities***, or download it free from www.ProLinguaAssociates.com.

❖ For "Whole-class Discussion" techniques and a suggested procedure, see the ***Supplementary Activities***, or download it free from www.prolinguaassociates.com.

❖ For "Applied Outside-class Interactions/Observations," see the ***Supplementary Activities***, or download it free from www.prolinguaassociates.com.

Part 3: Preparation for discussion for Unit 14

1. Do people from your culture usually smile in their pictures?
2. Do people from your culture smile at each other and strangers?
4. If you see a stranger and that person smiles at you, how do you feel?
5. Do you use emoticons when you send messages? What type do you use?
6. When you try to interpret someone's emotions, do you tend to look at their eyes or their mouths?
7. In ¶ 6-9, in general, were your answers more similar to the Chinese or Americans?
8. Look at the question in ¶ 12. How did you answer this?
9. Do you think what Brad Pitt did would be common or unusual in your country?
10. In ¶ 15 it talks about destiny. Is it important to you to be able to control your destiny? Explain.
11. Were you surprised to learn about the happiness level of the Indians living in the slums in ¶ 17?
12. This question is about ¶ 18-20. Think of a goal that you have that could make you happy. Tell us what it is.
13. This question is connected to the previous question. If you achieve that goal, which would be the reason for your happiness?
    a) I would be especially happy because it would make other people happy.
    b) I would be especially happy because it made me happy.
14. In general, are you happy these days? What is the reason?
15. Imagine that you had an interview for a good job, but you didn't get the job. Would you see this as a positive event that could lead you to greater happiness?
16. Do you tend to worry about whether or not you are happy?
17. After reading this textbook, would you rather live in a collectivist or individualist country? Explain.

Part 4: A technique for writing

Synthesize two sources in a paper.

In academic courses, assignments often require students to write papers in which they use information from more than one source. One common type of assignment is to use information from one source to explain the information in a second source.

This type of assignment will be practiced in this unit. You will read information about a cross-cultural problem. After that, you will write an essay in which you summarize the problem and use information from *Cultural Differences* to explain the cause of the problem.

Before starting your essay, you will analyze a model essay, in which the writer uses information from one source (*Cultural Differences*) to explain a problem that was described in a second source ("College Roommates").

Exercise 1

Read this passage, "College Roommates."

8

*College Roommates**

Hao

Josh

In September, Hao, an international student from Asia, arrived in the U.S. to enroll in a university. One of the first things that he did was to look for a place to live. He found an ad that had been posted by an American student, Josh, who was looking for a roommate who could share his two bedroom apartment. After meeting each other, they decided to become roommates.

For the first month of living together, Josh and Hao seemed to get along together well. However, after a while, they started to have problems. Josh began to notice that Hao would sometimes eat the groceries that Josh had bought. Hao was surprised one day to find a note in the refrigerator that said, "This shelf of food is Josh's. Don't take any unless you ask me." Another problem involved noise. Josh enjoyed playing loud music at night, and he asked Hao if the music bothered him. Hao took a deep breath and smiled but didn't say anything, so Josh thought it was fine.

Hao started to regret that he didn't have a roommate from his own country. He felt that Americans weren't clean because he noticed that Josh didn't do his laundry very often and sometimes smelled. He also was upset because he sometimes couldn't study because of Josh's loud music. To Hao, it seemed that Americans don't seem to care about other people.

Hao's life with Josh was so unhappy that, at the end of the term, he told Josh that he was going to move to a different apartment. Josh was shocked and asked Hao why he was leaving. Hao told him that he wanted to live a little closer to campus.

Source: The story came from Peggy Dustin's article, "College Roommates," *Culture Stories*, September 2010, page 8.
* The source of this passage, *Culture Stories*, is not available to the public.

Exercise 2

The model essay below uses information from *Cultural Differences* to explain the reasons why Hao and Josh had problems and misunderstandings. Read the essay and fill in the blanks with the words from the box.

Paragraphs 1-3

- One conflict that they
- things out (Kehe & Kehe, 2014).
- use non-verbal
- the refrigerator (Dustin, 2010).
- why their relationship was not successful.
- true feelings (Dustin, 2010).
- & Kehe (2014), collectivists such

Paragraphs 4-5

- Hao may need to be
- For example, he
- References
- the fundamental error
- should be prepared
- as roommates,

Challenges for Collectivists and Individualists Living Together

1) As more and more students see the value of an international education, there is now a greater chance that they will have opportunities to interact with people from different cultures. In order to have enjoyable and positive encounters, it's important that people understand each other's values and expectations. One place where cultures are mixing is at American colleges. Many international and American students view the chance to be roommates as an opportunity to learn more about another culture. Often these roommates develop close, lifetime friendships, but sometimes, because of cultural misunderstandings, the roommates end up with a negative impression of not only their roommate but also that person's culture in general. By analyzing the story of Josh and Hao, we can understand ____.

2) Josh, an American, and Hao, an Asian, were both students at an American college and decided to share an apartment. ______________________________ had concerned sharing food. Josh became upset because Hao would sometimes eat his food. As a result, Josh wrote a note saying directly that Hao should not take his food from _______ ______________________________. It is not surprising that they had this problem. According to Kehe ____ as Hao and individualists such as

Josh have different attitudes toward sharing. In a study of four-year-olds from Asia and America, researchers found that the Asian children were much more likely to share their food with a friend than the American children. In other words, sharing seems to be a norm that is common with collectivists but not so much with individualists. Because Josh's note directly accused Hao of taking his food, Hao probably felt as if he lost face. For collectivists, it's preferable for a criticism to be indirect.

3) Collectivists often ______________________ signals to express their opinions. Collectivists find these useful as a way to avoid direct confrontation with others. On the other hand, individualists usually spell ______________________________________ . This explains a second misunderstanding between Hao and Josh. When Josh asked Hao if his loud music bothered him, Hao used non-verbal signals, for example, by smiling and breathing deeply, to let Josh know that he did, indeed, not like the loud music. However, because Hao didn't express directly his opinion, in other words, didn't spell things out, Josh misunderstood Hao's ____ .

4) As a result of the bad experiences that Hao had with Josh, he developed a negative attitude toward Americans. He believed that Americans in general were not clean and weren't concerned about others because Josh wore dirty clothes and seemed to ignore Hao's feelings (Dustin, 2010). This is an example of ______________________________ of attribution. Hao is attributing Josh's bad behavior to weak points in Josh's in-group's personality, i.e., Americans. If Hao and Josh had been from the same in-group, Hao probably would have attributed Josh's bad habits specifically to a situation. _____________ might have thought that the washing machine didn't clean clothes properly, or that Josh didn't have enough money to wash his clothes more often.

5) Whenever students from individualist and collectivist cultures try to live ______ ______ there is potential for misunderstandings because of differences in cultural norms. Coincidentally, it is the differences in norms that make living with someone from another culture so interesting. If we can realize that there is a good reason why our roommates behave in a different manner and that they aren't acting differently because they are "strange" or have a bad personality, we might be more open to accepting each other. An individualist like Josh ________________________________ to not only listen to Hao, but to also look closely at his non-verbal signals. Along a similar line, a collectivist like ________ _________________ more direct in expressing his thoughts to Josh.

Dustin, P. (2010, September). "College Roommates." *Cultural Stories*, 8.

Kehe, D. & Kehe, P. (2014). *Cultural Differences*. Brattleboro, Vt.: Pro Lingua.

Exercise 3

Choose words from the box below and fill in the outline under the box. The outline is about the essay above, "Challenges for Collectivists and Individualists Living Together."

- ◆ Fundamental error of attribution ◆ Josh didn't want to share ◆ Dustin
- ◆ Hao attributed weak points to out-group's personality
- ◆ Using non-verbal signals ◆ Introduction and thesis statement
- ◆ Kehe & Kehe ◆ We should realize that there are good reasons for behavior.

Outline: Challenges for Collectivists and Individualists Living Together

1. (¶ 1)________________________________: Understanding why their relationship was not successful and why they had negative impressions.

2. (¶ 2) Sharing food
   a) ________________________________(Dustin)
   b) Research about four-year-olds sharing or not sharing (Kehe & Kehe)

3. (¶ 3) ________________________________
   a) Collectivists are used to avoiding confrontations, and individuals spell things out (________________)
   b) Hao smiled and breathed deeply but didn't spell things out (________________)

4. (¶ 4) ____
   a) Hao thought that Americans were not clean and unconcerned about others (Dustin)
   b) ____(Kehe & Kehe)

5. (¶ 5) Conclusion: ____

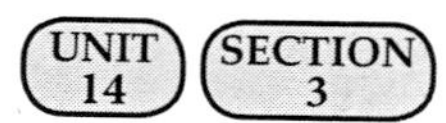

Exercise 4

1) Read the two articles below.
2) Choose <u>one</u> of the topic assignments.

12

Article One: *A Job in a Foreign Country**

Nine months ago, Brad's dream came true: He was hired to work at a company in an Asian country. When he first arrived in the country, he expected to stay for four years. However, he is so unhappy that he has decided to return to his hometown near Chicago at the end of the year.

One of the reasons why he wants to leave is because he feels like an outsider. Even though he has worked in this Asian country for nine months, nobody has invited him to their home. Also, he thinks that people laugh at him. For example, shoppers usually get a plastic bag from a grocery store to put their groceries in when they are shopping. Brad often re-uses one of these plastic bags to carry his lunch when he goes to work. Yesterday, a co-worker asked him what was in his bag, and when Brad told him that it was his lunch, the co-worker smiled and said that people usually only re-use these plastic bags for garbage. The other workers had been wondering why Brad was bringing his garbage to work.

Brad was also confused at his job. One of his first tasks was to hire a secretary, so he chose some applicants to interview. He found it difficult to find a well-qualified one because during the interviews, most of the applicants told him that they felt that they weren't as experienced as they should be with computers, or they said that they didn't think that they were very proficient in English, even though they seemed fluent to him. He wondered why they applied for the job if they didn't think that they were qualified.

Company meetings were often frustrating for him. He expected them to last about an hour, but often they took three or four. During that time, there were often long periods of quiet time, when nobody talked. It was rare for someone to offer an opinion, but instead they seemed to talk in general terms and without any specific goals.

Source: The story came from Peggy Dustin's article, "A Job in a Foreign Country," *Culture Stories*, September 2010, page 12.
*The source of this passage, *Culture Stories*, is not available to the public.

3

Article Two: *A Student in a Foreign Country**

Yu-Wen is an Asian student who has been studying in the U.S. for about two months. Although this is her first time to study abroad, her English skills are very good. At the beginning of the school term, she joined a club and met Amy, an American. Although they have become friends, they sometimes confuse each other.

Yu-Wen said that she'd like to meet more Americans, so Amy invited her to a party at Mike's apartment. During the party, Yu-Wen stood in the corner by herself. Sometimes, people would approach her and talk, and she would smile but not say much. Mike asked Amy, "Why doesn't Yu-Wen walk around and socialize with people?"

Amy answered, "In my opinion, she is just shy, but I think she is having a good time because she is always smiling."

The next day, Yu-Wen called her sister in her country and talked about her life in the U.S. She said, "Americans sometimes make me feel uncomfortable. Last week, I got in line to wait for a bus, and a man who was in front of me looked at me and smiled. He seemed rather strange. And at the party last night, I met a girl, and the first thing that she said was that she loved my earrings. I don't think that she was sincere. They are really cheap ones. I also talked to a guy named Joe. He started bragging about how good he was with computers, and he could help me if I had any problems. I didn't like him. His opinion of himself was too good."

Soon after the party, Amy asked Yu-Wen if she'd like to have dinner with her and Joe the next Saturday. Yu-Wen just smiled. Then Amy said, "Great! I'll pick you up at 7:00." Yu-Wen really didn't want to go, so Saturday afternoon she told Amy that she had another appointment.

Source: The story came from Peggy Dustin's article, "A Student in a Foreign Country," *Culture Stories*, August 2010, page 3.
*The source of this passage, *Culture Stories*, is not available to the public.

Topic 1 Assignment

Write an essay in which you explain why Brad had problems. Use information from ***Cultural Differences*** to support your ideas.

Topic 2 Assignment

Write an essay in which you explain the causes of the misunderstanding that Yu-Wen, Amy, Mike and/or Joe had. Use information from ***Cultural Differences*** to support your ideas.

You can organize your essay in this way:

- an introduction and thesis statement
- a summary of one problem that Brad or Yu-Wen had
- a paraphrase of information from *Cultural Differences* to explain why they had the problem (You can use information from all of *Cultural Differences*.)
- a summary of a second problem that Brad or Yu-Wen had
- a paraphrase of information from *Cultural Differences* to explain why they had the problem
- *(optional)* a summary of another problem and the reason for the problem
- a conclusion in which you explain what you learned from this and/or give some recommendations
- "References" at the end of the paper

References

Argyle, M., Henderson, M., Bond, M., Iizuka, Y., & Contarello, A. (1986). Cross-cultural variations in relationship rules. *International Journal of Psychology* 21, 287-315.

Asch, S. E. (1956). Studies of independence and conformity: A minority of one against a unanimous majority. *Psychological Monographs*, 70, (9), 1–70.

Barnlund, D., & S. Araki. (1985). Intercultural Encounters: the management of compliments by Japanese and Americans. *Journal of Cross-Cultural Psychology*. 16. 9-26

Bartimus, T. (2002, May 12).WWBPD: What would Brad Pitt do? Life after college is great unknown. *Seattle Times*.

Berry, J., Poortinga, Y., Segall, M., & Dasen, P. (1992). *Cross-Cultural Psychology: research and application*. New York: Cambridge University Press

Birch, L., & Billman, J .(1986). Preschool children's food sharing with friends and acquaintances. *Child Development*, 57, 387-395.

Biswas-Diener, R., & Diener, E. (2001) Making the best of a bad situation: Satisfaction in the slums of Calcutta. *Social Indicators Research*, 55, 329–352.

Boesch, E. (1994). First Experience in Thailand. In W. Lonner & R. Malpass (Eds.). *Psychology and Culture* (pp. 47-52). Boston: Allyn & Bacon.

Bond, M., & Venus, C. K. (1991). Resistance to group or personal insults in an ingroup or outgroup context. *International Journal of Psychology*, 26, 83-94.

Bond, M., Wan, K., Leung, K., & Giacalone, R. (1985). How are responses to verbal insults related to cultural collectivism and power distance? *Journal of Cross-Cultural Psychology* 16, 111-127

Bond, R. & Smith, P. (1996). Culture and conformity: A meta-analysis of studies using Asch's 1952b, 1956) line judgment task. *Psychological Bulletin*, 119, 111-137.

Brandt, V. (1974). Skiing cross-culturally. *Current Anthropology*, 15, 64-66

Brislin, R. (1994). Preparing to live and work elsewhere. In W. Lonner & R. Malpass (Eds.). *Psychology and Culture* (pp. 239-244). Boston: Allyn & Bacon, 1994.

Brislin, R. (2001) Intercultural Contact and Communication. In Loeb-Adler, L., & Gielen, U. (Eds.), *Cross-Cultural Topics in Psychology*. (213-227). Westport,CT: Greenwood/Praeger.

Buss, D. (1994) Mate preferences in 37 cultures." In W. Lonner, & R. Malpass, (Eds), *Psychology and Culture* (pp. 197-201) Boston: Allyn and Bacon.

Carson, J. & Nelson, G.. (1994). Writing Groups: Cross-Cultural Issues. *Journal of Second Language Writing* 3, 17-30.

Cushner, K., & Brislin, R. (1996). *Intercultural Interactions*: A practical guide (2nd ed.). Thousand Oaks: Sage.

DeCapua, A., & Wintergerst, A. (2004). *Crossing Cultures in the Language Classroom*. Ann Arbor: The University of Michigan Press.

Diaz-Guerrero, R. (1979). The development of coping style. *Human Development*, 22, 320-331

Frager, R. (1970). Conformity and anti-conformity in Japan. *Journal of Personality and Social Psychology*, 15, 203-210.

Gardiner, H. (2001). Child and Adolescent Development: Cross-Cultural Perspectives. In L. Adler, & U. Gielen (Eds.) *Cross-Cultural Topics in Psychology* (2nd ed., pp. 63-80) Westport, CT: Praeger.

Haar, B. & Krahe, B. (1999). Strategies for resolving interpersonal conflicts in adolescence. *Journal of Cross-Cultural Psychology*, 30. 667-682

Hall, E. (1976). *Beyond culture*. Garden City, NY: Doubleday / Anchor.

Haruki, Y., Shigehisa, T., Nedate, K., Wajima, M., & Ogawa, R. (1984). Effects of alien-reinforcement and its combined type on learning behavior and efficacy in relation to personality. *International Journal of Psychology*, 19, 527-545.

Hofsted, G. (1980). *Culture's consequences: International differences in work-related values*. Beverly Hills: Sage.

Hollaway, S., Kashiwagi, K, Hess, R, & Azuma, H. (1986). Causal attributions by Japanese and American mothers and children about performance in mathematics. *International Journal of Psychology*, 21, 269-86.

Iyengar, S., & Lepper, M. (1999). Rethinking the value of choice: A cultural perspective on intrinsic motivation. *Journal of Personality and Social Psychology*, 76, 349-366.

Janaro, R., & Altschuler, T. (2003). *The art of being human* (7th ed.). New York: Pearson Longman.

Janis, I. (1983). The role of social support in adherence to stressful decisions. *American Psychologist*. 38, 143-160.

Kidder, L. (1992) Requirements for being "Japanese." *International Journal of Intercultural Relations*. 16. 383-393.

Kim, H. S., & Markus, H. R. (1999). Deviance or uniqueness, harmony or conformity? A cultural analysis. *Journal of Personality and Social Psychology*, 77, 785-800.

Kitayam, Shinobu, Hazel Markus, and Masaru Kurokawa. (2000). Culture, Emotion, and Well-being: Good feelings in Japan and the United States. *Cognition and Emotions*, 14, 93-124

Koenig, A., & Dean, K. (2011). Cross-Cultural Differences and Similarities in Attribution. In K. Keith (Ed.) *Cross-Cultural Psychology: Contemporary Themes and Perspectives* (pp. 475-493) Oxford: Wiley-Blackwell.

Koren, M. (2010, December 7). Cultural differences explain emotional expression. *The Review*. From http://www.udreview.com/editorial/cultural-differences-explain-emotional-expression-1.1822290#.UPLxxW_hpLZ

Laungani, Pittu. (2007) *Understanding Cross-Cultural Psychology*. London: Saga.

Leung, K., & Park, H. (1986). Effects of interactional goal on choice allocation rule: a cross-cultural study. *Organizational Behavior and Human Decisions Process*, 37, 111-120.

Levine , R. V. (2003).The kindness of strangers. American Scientist, 91, 226-233.

Levine, R.V., & Bartlett, K. 1984. Pace of life, punctuality, and coronary heart disease in six countries. *Journal of Cross-Cultural Psychology*, 15: 233-255.

Lu, L., & Gilmour, R. (2004). Culture and conceptions of happiness: Individual oriented and social oriented SWB. *Journal of Happiness Studies*, 5, 269–291.

Matsumoto, D. (1991). Cultural influences on facial expressions of emotion. *Southern Communication Journal*, 56, 128-137.

Matsumoto, D. (2000). *Culture and Psychology: People Around the World*. Belmont, CA: Wadsworth.

Matsumoto, D. (2006). Are cultural differences in emotion regulation mediated by personality traits? *Journal of Cross-Cultural Psychology*, 37, 421-437.

Moghaddam, F., Taylor, D. & Wright, S. (1993). *Social Psychology in Cross-Cultural Perspectives.* New York: W.H. Freeman.

Morris, M., & Peng, K. (1994). Culture and cause: American and Chinese attribution for social and physical events. *Journal of personality and social psychology*, 67, 949-971.

Rao, N., & Sunita, S. (1999). Cultural influences on sharer and recipient behavior. *Journal of Cross-Cultural Psychology*, 30, 219-239

Science Daily (2007) Culture Is Key To Interpreting Facial Emotions. From http://www.sciencddaily. com/release/2007/04/070404162321.htm.

Segall, M., Dasen. H., Berry, J., & Poortinga. Y. (1999). *Human Behavior in Global Perspective.* Boston: Allyn and Bacon.

Shiraev, E., & Levy, D. (2001). *Introduction to Cross-Cultural Psychology*. Boston: Allyn and Bacon.

Simons, D., Irwin, D., & Drinnien, A. (1987). *Psychology-The Search for Understanding.* New York: West Publishing Company.

Smith, P., & M. Bond. (1994). *Social Psychology Across Cultures.* Boston: Allyn and Bacon.

Spiegel, A. (Producer) (2012, Nov. 12). Struggle for smarts? How eastern and western cultures tackle learning [Radio series episode]. *In Morning Edition*. NPR. Retrieved from http://www.npr.org/blogs/health/2012/11/12/164793058/struggle-for-smarts-how-eastern-and-western-cultures-tackle-learning

Stevenson, H.., & Lee, S., Chen, C., Stigler, J., Hsu, C., & Kitamura, S. (1990). Context of achievement. *Monographs of the Society for Research in Child Development*, 55, 1-120.

Stipek, D. (1998). Differences between Americans and Chinese in the Circumstances Evoking Pride, Shame, and Guilt. *Journal of Cross-Cultural Psychology*, 29, 616-629.

Suh, E. M., & Oishi, S. (2002). Subjective well-being across cultures. In W. J. Lonner, D. L. Dinnel, S. A. Hayes, & D. N. Sattler (Eds.), *Online Readings in Psychology and Culture* (Unit 7, Chapter 1), (http://www.wwu.edu/~culture), Center for Cross-Cultural Research, Western Washington University, Bellingham, Washington USA

Triandis, H. (1994a). Culture and social behavior. In W. Lonner & R. Malpass (Eds.). *Psychology and Culture* (pp. 169-173). Boston: Allyn & Bacon.

Triandis, H. (1994b). *Culture and Social Behavior*. New York: McGraw-Hill, 1994.

Triandis, H. C. (1990). Cross-cultural studies of individualism and collectivism. In J. J. Berman (Ed.), *Cross-cultural perspectives, Nebraska Symposium on Motivation 1989*: 41–133. Lincoln: University of Nebraska Press

Triandis, H., Bontempo, R., Villareal, M., Asai, M., & Lucca, N. (1988). Individualism and collectivism: Crosscultural perspectives on self-ingroup relationships. *Journal of Personality and Social Psychology*, 54, 323-338.

Uchida, Y., Norasakkunkit, V., & Kitayama, S. (2004). Cultural constructions of happiness: Theory and empirical evidence. Journal of Happiness Studies, 5, 223-239.

Whittaker, J., & Whittaker, S. (1972). A cross-cultural study of geocentrism. *Journal of Cross-Cultural Psychology*, 3, 417-421.

Yang, W. (2011, May 16). Paper tigers: what happens to all the Asian-American overachievers when the test-taking ends? *New York*, 44, 22-95.

Other books from Pro Lingua

AT THE HIGH-INTERMEDIATE AND ADVANCED LEVELS

Also by David and Peggy Kehe

- Discussion Strategies — Carefully structured pair and small group work at the advanced-intermediate level. Excellent preparation for students who will participate in academic or professional work that requires effective participation in discussion and seminars.

- The Grammar Review Book — This easy-to-use book is designed for anyone who has learned English by ear and who needs to write grammatically. The students learn to recognize and correct common, fossilized errors through a carefully sequenced series of exercises.

- Writing Strategies — There are two volumes in this student-centered essay-writing course. Each introduces four types of essay, in four rhetorical modes, following a writing-editing process, a careful sequence of steps from preparing the first draft to writing the final essay. The four modes in Book One at the High-Intermediate level are Description, Narration, Exposition, and Comparison and Contrast. The modes in Book Two at the Advanced level are Process, Cause and Effect, Extended Definition, and Argumentation. This essay writing is augmented by two supplementary activities in the second and third sections of each book.

  Fluency Writing. In pairs and triads, the students exchange information on a contemporary topic. They finish the activity by summarizing in writing what they have discussed.

  Grammar Problems and Terminology. In this section, the students review those pesky grammar problems that always show up in the process of putting thoughts into grammatically accurate sentences. These are recommended if needed at specific points in the essay-writing process.

Other books that may be useful to High-Intermediate to Advanced Students

Full descriptions of these PHOTOCOPYABE books with sample materials are available at our webstore: www.ProLinguaAssociates.com

- Pronunciation Practice: The Sounds of North American English
- Grammar Practice: Worksheets for 212 Interactive Grammar Activities
- The Modal Book: The American English Modal System
- A Phrasal Verb Affair: Over 200 Phrasal Verbs Used in a Soap Opera
- Getting A Fix on Vocabulary: Prefixes, Suffixes, Bases, Compounds
- Business Communication Strategies – in the International Business World
- What's Ahead? Transitioning from Adult Education to a Career
- Teaching in the United States – a handbook for International Educators

Pro Lingua Associates ❖ PO Box 1348, Brattleboro, VT 05301 ❖ 800-366-4775